Octavia Hill
and the
Social Housing Debate

Essays and Letters by

Octavia Hill

Edited by
Robert Whelan

First published February 1998

The IEA Health and Welfare Unit
2 Lord North St
London SW1P 3LB

© The IEA Health and Welfare Unit 1998

ISBN 0-255 36431-8

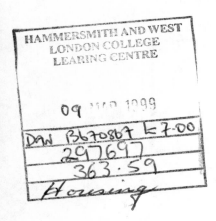
Typeset by the IEA Health and Welfare Unit
in Bookman 10 point
Printed in Great Britain by
St Edmundsbury Press
Blenheim Industrial Park, Newmarket Road
Bury St Edmunds, Suffolk, IP33 3TU

297697

Contents

The Authors

Octavia Hill (1838-1912) was born in Wisbech into a family with a radical campaigning tradition on both sides. Her maternal grandfather, Thomas Southwood Smith, was a pioneer of sanitary reform. Her father edited a radical newspaper promoting Robert Owen's socialist ideas. Following the bankruptcy of her father and his complete nervous breakdown, Octavia moved to London with her mother and sisters. She helped her mother with the management of a workshop in which children from a Ragged School were taught to make dolls' furniture, then trained as a copyist of Old Master paintings under John Ruskin. In 1864 Ruskin put up the money to acquire the leases of three houses in Marylebone which he put under Octavia's management. She developed a style of managing working-class housing which put as much emphasis on improving the tenants as the tenements. Other supporters purchased property for her to manage, or gave her the management of their existing property. By the mid-1870s Octavia estimated that she was responsible for 3,000 tenants. The success of her methods led the Ecclesiastical Commissioners to place large estates under her care. She did pioneering work in the movement to preserve open spaces and was one of the founders of the National Trust in 1895. She was a founder member of the Charity Organisation Society and maintained its opposition to state welfare until her death. She was a member of the Royal Commission on the Poor Laws which met from 1905-1908. At the time of her death Octavia was estimated to be managing about 1,900 flats and houses, but she refused all requests to form an organisation to perpetuate her work.

Robert Whelan is the Assistant Director of the Health and Welfare Unit at the IEA. His publications include *Mounting Greenery*, IEA Education Unit 1988; *Choices in Childbearing*, Committee on Population and the Economy 1992; *Broken Homes and Battered Children* and *Teaching Sex in Schools*, Family Education Trust 1994 and 1995; *Making a Lottery of Good Causes* (with Roger Cummins) and *The Corrosion of Charity*, IEA, 1995 and 1996; and *The Cross and the Rainforest* (with Paul Haffner and Joseph Kirwan), Acton Institute and Eerdmans, 1996.

Foreword

Octavia Hill's ideas can be found at the heart of most of today's social policy pre-occupations.

Her philosophy was to develop the potential and self-sufficiency of all those around her. Her aims were to find employment for young people, to improve education and opportunities for the poor, especially women, to find a way to provide rented housing without subsidy for those with low incomes, to improve housing standards, to create cleaner air and to maintain open spaces in the heart of the industrialised city. However, what marks her out from so many radical intellectuals is that she was able to give concrete expression to her theories.

Octavia Hill's housing work seems increasingly relevant in the 1990s as housing managers struggle to run estates whose residents are heavily disadvantaged by every social indicator. The current emphasis is on Housing Plus, an approach under which housing association landlords do more than just provide homes which people on low incomes can afford. Housing Associations are finding ways of helping to revitalise communities by initiating training, employment, childcare, leisure and many other projects with their tenants, which will help to improve their opportunities and reduce the poverty which many housing association tenants face.

Two years ago we decided to begin each Committee of Management meeting of the Octavia Hill Housing Trust with a reading from something either by or about Octavia. There is no danger of running out of readings as Octavia had so much to say which is relevant, not only to today's big issues, but to the day-to-day problems caused by poor administration and shortage of time.

It is strange that she is so much less well-known than other eminent Victorians. Perhaps this is due to her commitment to operating on a small scale, and to her belief that she should only set a pattern for others to learn from and develop. The large organisations which memorialised some of her contemporaries were not for Octavia. Indeed the Housing Trust which she founded, and which still flourishes in London one hundred years on, only took her name into its title a few years ago.

The publication of Octavia Hill's writings by the IEA is timely. The climate of late twentieth century Britain looks for better ways of sustaining individuals, the economy and the environment. On all of these important issues Octavia Hill's writings serve as a fresh and inspirational source for new policies and action.

Debby Ounsted
Chief Executive, Octavia Hill Housing Trust

Acknowledgements

Chapter 4, 'Selections from Octavia Hill's Letters to Fellow-Workers', is reproduced, with permission, from the letters in the collection of the Westminster City Archive. Chapter 8, 'Advice to Fellow-Workers in Edinburgh', is reproduced, with permission, from Octavia Hill's manuscript which is preserved in the archive of the Edinburgh Social Union, held in the Edinburgh Room of the Central Library in Edinburgh. Chapter 9, 'Housing Difficulties', is reproduced, with permission, from the copy held in the Goldsmith's Library of Economic Literature, University of London Library. Like so many authors, I am indebted to the helpful and friendly staff at the London Library. Debby Ounsted, Chief Executive of the Octavia Hill Housing Trust, supplied information about housing associations in general and her own in particular. David Gladstone advised on the history of local government, and useful suggestions were made by the anonymous participants in the IEA's refereeing process. Allen and Elizabeth Mills helped with proof-reading. Finally I would like to thank Peter Clayton of the Octavia Hill Society for his unfailing enthusiasm and support. The Society can be contacted at The Octavia Hill Birthplace Museum Trust, 1 South Brink Place, Wisbech, Cambs PE13 1JE.

Almost the worst house, if the household be wisely governed,
is better than ever so costly a one ill-managed

Octavia Hill

Editor's Introduction

Robert Whelan

I N 1887 a service was held in Westminster Abbey to commemorate Queen Victoria's Golden Jubilee. Only three women were invited to attend in their own right: Florence Nightingale, Josephine Butler and Octavia Hill.

Florence Nightingale has long since passed into the pantheon of great historical figures and Josephine Butler is still remembered for her campaigns against the oppression of women. Octavia Hill, on the other hand, has been almost completely forgotten. If she is remembered at all, it is as one of the co-founders of the National Trust, an organisation which was only one among many of Octavia's interests, and certainly not the most important. She was one of those curious people who make an enormous impression upon their contemporaries and then seem to sink from view.

Octavia Hill was born in 1838 in Wisbech into a family with a tradition of support for radical causes on both sides. Her maternal grandfather was Dr Thomas Southwood Smith, the pioneer of sanitary reform who was later to become one of the Commissioners of the first Board of Health. Her mother Caroline was an educational theorist and teacher who championed the methods of J. Pestalozzi, 'the children's friend'. As a result of one of her magazine articles Caroline was contacted by James Hill, a widower looking for a governess for his children. She accepted the position, and they were soon afterwards married.

James shared the interest of his wife's family in reforming movements, and in particular wanted to promote Robert Owen's brand of socialism. He set up, together with Caroline, a pioneering infant school in Wisbech, based on Owen's New Lanark school, and founded an East Anglian newspaper called *The Star of the East* to promote radical ideas. He attempted to set up a co-operative commune, again imitating Owen, and founded the United Advancement Society, but he became seriously over-extended financially as a result of his involvement with radical causes and was declared bankrupt in 1840. Soon afterwards

1

James Hill experienced a severe nervous breakdown. As a result of medical advice he never lived with his family again, with the result that, from her earliest years, Octavia was brought up in a fatherless household.

Caroline Hill moved around the country with her children, trying to establish the family somewhere where they would have means of supporting themselves. Eventually they settled in London in 1851, where Caroline Hill was appointed manager of The Ladies' Guild, a co-operative workshop set up by the Christian Socialist movement to provide employment for un-skilled women and girls. Still only 14, Octavia was also appointed as the manager of a group of children from a ragged school who were originally employed to paint glass tables. She became deeply involved with the lives of her young charges, discovering at first hand the terrible conditions in which the poor of London lived, and she did everything she could to improve the quality of their lives. She organised them to contribute to a common fund from which they would buy food to prepare a nourishing midday meal, for less than they were paying before for poor-quality food, and she took them on outings to the countryside and the British Museum. However, following the closure of the Ladies' Guild in 1856, Octavia was in urgent need of alternative employment.

Octavia's Christian Socialism

Whilst living in London Octavia had fallen under the influence of the Rev. F.D. Maurice, the founder of Christian Socialism, who was chaplain at Lincoln's Inn. She was a frequent attender at his services and went into raptures over his sermons, which most people found incomprehensible. Although brought up as a nonconformist (the Hills were Unitarians) Octavia was baptised and confirmed in the Church of England by Maurice, together with her sisters Miranda and Emily. The intensity of Octavia's religious experience at this time, in which worship of the Almighty was inextricably bound up with social reform and concern for the poor, was to have the most profound influence on the future direction of her life.

Maurice offered Octavia the post of secretary to the women's classes at the Working Men's College in Red Lion Square, at a salary of £26 a year. At the same time John Ruskin offered to train her as a copyist, making accurate reproductions of old master paintings. Ruskin was the most influential art critic of the day who shared the Christian Socialists' concern with social reform. He had met Octavia when visiting the Ladies' Guild workshop and Octavia, who was prone as a teenager to hero-worship, put him up on the pedestal beside Maurice. Ruskin was already teaching at the Working Men's College when Octavia was engaged as secretary, and he seems to have spotted in Octavia a possible vehicle for his own ideas on social reform. Although Octavia took her artistic work very seriously, and saw a career for herself in the arts,[1] Ruskin was more perceptive. 'If you devote yourself to human expression, I know how it will be', he told her. 'There will be an end of art for you. You will say "*hang* drawing!! I must go to help people."'[2] Octavia assured him that it would not be so. As her biographer Gillian Darley observed, it was one of the few occasions when she was completely wrong.

The Family Tradition

Octavia had grown up in a household in which the serious topics of social reform were the staple of family conversation. Inspired by the example of Dr Southwood Smith's courageous campaign against the evils of cholera and other contagious diseases, his daughter and grand-daughters accepted it, almost as family tradition, that they should be in the vanguard of movements to improve the lot of the poor. According to Octavia's beloved sister Miranda: 'At the age of 14 the condition of the poor, the efforts of the working people by co-operation and by their Trades Unions to improve their condition, occupied her thoughts'.[3] The intensity of her religious fervour under the influence of Maurice and the Christian Socialists only increased her conviction that she was under an absolute moral duty to engage in whatever course of action might be open to her to improve the lot of others. The question was, in the vast and vibrant field of philanthropic activities which formed such an important part of the culture of Victorian England, which particular cause would she make her own?

In 1859 Octavia attended a meeting to launch the Ladies' Sanitary Association. Her grandfather, Dr Southwood Smith, was there together with his friend the Earl of Shaftesbury (the 'poor man's earl'), and they all listened to an inspiring speech by Charles Kingsley. Kingsley told them that it was no good looking to the government to carry out the vital work of sanitary reform because it was beyond the power of government to accomplish the necessary tasks. According to the account of his speech which Octavia gave to her sister Miranda, this was because of the way in which small houses which were being used for working-class accommodation were passing into the hands of landlords who cared little for the welfare of their tenants. Kingsley appealed to ladies to go 'not only to the occupiers, but to the possessors of the houses, and influence people of "our own class"'.[4] By instilling the doctrine of sanitary reform in such landlords and their tenants, Kingsley told them, lady visitors could save four out of every five children who died annually:

> It is in the power, I believe, of any woman in this room to save three or four lives, human lives, during the next six months. It is in your power, ladies, and it is so easy.

The impact upon Octavia of such a speech, building, as it did, on the work of her own grandfather, must have been immense. Later in the same year F.D. Maurice lent her a copy of a book about Ellen Ranyard's Bible Women, called *The Missing Link*. This also impressed her by its account of the way in which the Bible Women did an immense amount of good by visiting and befriending the poor, but without giving them handouts in a way which would have undermined their self-reliance. According to Octavia's account:

> They are quite poor women, sent by ladies to sell Bibles... They have reached the very lowest class, seen and helped them in their homes. They give nothing away, but get people to buy beds and clothes, for which they pay gradually. They encouraged women to take a pride in keeping their children and homes neat; and living among them, can do so much.[5]

The attraction to Octavia of an approach to helping the poor which was based on befriending and advising them, without free gifts, whilst at the same time striving to bring rich and poor together, became obvious a few years later when she embarked on the work which was to make her so famous that she came to be regarded as one of the formative influences on the Victorian era.

The Tenants Nobody Else Would Touch

In 1864 Octavia decided to set herself up as a landlady:

> I have long been wanting to gather near us my friends among the poor, in some house arranged for their health and convenience, in fact

a small private model lodging-house, where I may know everyone, and do something towards making their lives healthier and happier.[6]

The money was to be provided by John Ruskin, who had become a wealthy man on the death of his father. However, Octavia soon found that opening a model lodging-house was a more difficult matter than she had anticipated. Whenever she found a suitable property, the owners would withdraw from negotiations when they discovered what she intended to do with it. 'Where *are* the poor to live?' she asked an agent in frustration. 'I don't know, but they must keep off the St John's Wood Estate', was his reply.[7] It soon became obvious that she would have to take over an existing tenement building and work with both the house and the tenants in whatever condition they came to her. A friend drew her attention to three houses for sale in Paradise Place, a court near her own home in Marylebone which was so rough it was known locally as Little Hell. The asking price for the 56-year leases was £750, which Ruskin agreed to pay, on condition that the properties could be managed to show a five per cent return on capital investment. This was not because he needed the money, but to encourage others with capital to invest in working-class housing.

And so it was that Octavia found herself the landlady, not of a model lodging-house into which she could put her special 'friends among the poor', but of three stinking run-down tenements bursting at the seams with roughs and rowdies.[8] Ever ready to see the hand of divine providence at work, Octavia soon took it to be her special mission to work in just this way. Let others build model dwellings and fill them with members of the respectable working classes: she would take the very worst elements and make them better (see p. 85). The 'Octavia Hill system', as it became known, was summed up by Lord Salisbury as: 'to improve the tenants with the tenements'.[9] Octavia outlined her method (a term she preferred to 'system') in dealing with what she described as 'the destructive class of tenants' to the Royal Commission on the Housing of the Working Classes in 1884:

> The difficulty with these people is not financial, but moral; and, therefore, I know nothing for them but some individual power and watchfulness. They must be trained... You may have a destructive drunken man, whom neither Sir Sydney Waterlow's, nor any other society, would take into their buildings at all, for he will not conform to the rules; the only way that I know of getting hold of him is buying

up the house in which he is, exactly as it is, and making him profit by his own care... I say to them, 'You must either do better or you must leave; which is it to be?'[10]

In the first three chapters of this book, which first appeared as magazine articles, Octavia explained the nuts and bolts of her approach. When she took over a property she would take whatever steps were necessary to make it sound and hygienic, sorting out drains and dustbins and clearing refuse from the yards, but there would be no more improvements until she was sure that the tenants were 'capable of valuing and not abusing them' (p. 68). 'Steady and gradual improvement of the people and of the houses, without selection of the former or sudden reconstruction of the latter'[11] was her motto.

Octavia had a conception of the landlord/tenant relationship which verged on the sacred, and imposed the most serious duties on both parties. The tenant was under an absolute moral obligation to pay the rent each week; the landlord was under an equally pressing obligation to keep the property in good repair. When these primary functions had been discharged, other good things could flow from the relationship. Without this basic bond of trust, nothing else could happen.

Octavia set herself to improve the lives of her tenants in many ways. She encouraged thrift and industry by starting savings banks, and by providing work for unemployed men, whenever possible, in her properties. Older girls would be paid to clean the common parts—the landlady's responsibility. She organised lessons and singing classes for the children, and a working group for married women, who all met in the converted stable behind her house in Nottingham Place, Marylebone. She organised Christmas parties and summer outings, flower shows, cadet corps and working men's clubs. But she did everything in a way which would encourage self-improvement and discourage dependency:

> [M]y strongest endeavours were to be used to rouse habits of industry and effort, without which they must finally sink—and with which they might render themselves independent of me, except as a friend and leader (p. 44).

The one thing she would not do was give them money or allow them to run up rent arrears. Throughout her life Octavia had a horror of careless charity, which encouraged sloth and imprudence in the poor, and locked them into a condition of permanent dependency. She insisted that her way was best because she treated the poor as she would treat friends of her own class:

> I should give them any help I could, such as I might offer without insult to other friends—sympathy in their distresses; advice, help and counsel in their difficulties; introductions that might be of use to them; means of education; visits to the country; a loan of books; a bunch of flowers brought on purpose; an invitation to any entertainment, in a room built at the back of my own house... I am convinced that one of the evils of much that is done for the poor springs from the want of delicacy felt, and courtesy shown, towards them, and that we cannot beneficially help them in any spirit different to that in which we help those who are better off (p. 69).[12]

A System Without Rules

Octavia did not regard herself as a theorist, and had an almost pathological dislike of anything that looked like a system, as she believed that no system, however subtle, could respond to the individual needs of the poor. The 'Octavia Hill system', therefore, which those interested in social housing were soon referring to, had remarkably few rules. Indeed, she told the Royal Commission in 1884 that there was only one: no sub-letting. It was common at the time for a poor family to take one room, and then sub-let a corner of it to someone even poorer than themselves. Octavia would not tolerate this as she could not have the same sort of relationship with—one might say the same control over—the tenant who was not responsible to her. In spite of her insistence on 'the extreme importance of enforcing the punctual payment of rents' (p. 79), and her claim that she 'never allowed a second week's rent to become due' (p. 53) without starting proceedings for eviction, she was more flexible than she pretended even here, sometimes allowing arrears to build up if the tenants were depositors in her Penny Bank.[13]

Octavia would put out immediately any tenants leading 'clearly immoral lives' (p. 53)[14]—by which she presumably meant prostitutes—but her attitude towards alcoholics was more flexible. She would tolerate those who were really trying to conquer their addiction, but she might decide that this or that tenant was just causing too many problems for the neighbours and would have to go (see p. 118 for an account of the eviction of a tenant with *delirium tremens*). It was a tremendous authority to be able to 'say to this man "Go", and... to that one, "Stay"', and Octavia recognised this.[15] She took her responsibilities extremely seriously, but she had no doubt that certain characteristics like industry, thrift and sobriety were preferable to others like drunkenness, sloth and loutishness. She saw it as her clear duty to encourage the former and discourage the latter through the power which she possessed as a landlady.

The Octavia Hill system, therefore, was based on deeply-held convictions, which might be variable in the way in which they were put into effect. She insisted that it had been '*worked out*' in practice and not '*thought out* in the study' (p. 69). For this reason she always refused to act through a committee or to form any sort of organisation (see p. 119). She needed to have the absolute discretion to do as she saw best. Fortunately, it seemed to have good results.[16]

The Growth of the Work

As the awareness of her work grew, so she found that more and more people wanted to put working-class properties under her care. In 1866, the year after she had officially taken over the management of Paradise Place, John Ruskin made his second purchase for Octavia. He paid £2,880 to purchase the freeholds of five houses in Freshwater Place in Marylebone and the house on the corner with Old Marylebone Road which backed onto it. Because he owned the freehold of the site, Ruskin was able to demolish some of the buildings to create a little patch of land which Octavia turned into a playground. In view of her spectacular later work in the campaign to preserve open spaces this was a significant step (see Chapter Two). Then, in 1869, Octavia began her involvement with Barrett's Court, between Oxford Street and Wigmore Street. The Countess of Ducie purchased six ten-roomed houses for £7,000 and Mrs Stopford Brooke purchased another five. She tells the story of her work there in Chapter Three.

By this stage the work had progressed beyond the point at which Octavia could manage all of the houses herself, and she had begun to gather round herself the band of fellow-workers who would carry it forward. Some of these were volunteers and some were paid, but Octavia made no distinction in terms of what she expected of them. Hester and Julia Sterling, two sisters who admired Octavia, purchased Walmer Street and Walmer Place in Marylebone for Emma Cons to manage. Emma Cons, later famous as the founder of the Old Vic, was a working-class woman who needed to support herself, so she was paid. However, she was Octavia's most trusted first lieutenant, able to operate with little or no supervision. Henrietta Rowlands, on the other hand, who was later Henrietta Barnett of Toynbee Hall, had a private income and worked as a volunteer.

Octavia found herself being offered the management of more and more property, spread around London, but she would not take on any house or court until she felt she had the right person to manage it. In fact, she always insisted that the only constraint on her work was shortage of the right people, not lack of money (p. 84). She held a list of donors waiting to buy houses for her to manage and, when she found the right property and the right person to manage it, she would put them together with the donor she felt was most likely to take an interest in that particular venture.

Although Octavia took on properties a house at a time or a court at a time, by concentrating the interest of her donors on certain streets, she was able to build up a sufficient number of properties to influence the tone of the area by her management. Her activities in Notting Hill, which she describes in Chapter Nine, illustrate this. She began by taking on five houses next to the church hall at the request of the vicar. 'If much good were to be done there, more property must be acquired', she told her fellow-workers in the circular letter for 1899. This was followed by the purchase of 17 houses by 'a friend' (p. 122). By 1902 she was managing 45 properties in St Katherine's Street (now Wilsham Street) and by 1910 this had risen to 63, with about 100 houses in the Notting Hill area under her control.

However the event which was to lead to the largest expansion of her work occurred in 1884 when Octavia was asked to take over the management of 48 houses in Deptford for the Ecclesiastical Commissioners (now the Church Commissioners), followed by several courts in Southwark and another 78 houses in Deptford in January 1885. Although she never had any official position with the Ecclesiastical Commissioners, beyond managing property as and when requested, Octavia began to exert a great influence over the way in which they operated. She persuaded them that it was undesirable that they should sell leases of 80 or 90 years on their properties, so that for long periods they had no effective control over them, as this resulted in many houses being managed in a way which reflected no credit on the church. She also persuaded them that, when leases fell in, they should try to rehabilitate old properties rather than demolish them (a favourite theme of Octavia's) and that, if reconstruction were absolutely necessary, they should build at least some cottages to replace the old houses, and not use every site for blocks of tenements.

She won them over completely. The Commissioners decided that instead of selling long leases on properties they would retain direct control—and handed it all over to Octavia to manage for them. In 1901 she was asked to take over 50 houses in Southwark (at four days notice) and 160 houses in Lambeth on the same day; in 1903 the leases fell in on between 500 and 600 houses in Walworth; and in 1904 she took over the Lambeth Estate near Waterloo Station, housing 256 families.[17]

Although it was not possible, owing to high land values in central London, to give up building tenement blocks entirely, the Commissioners built some cottages in Southwark and Westminster. They also gave Octavia, on very favourable terms, leases on plots in Southwark where she built the Red Cross and White Cross Cottages, together with their garden which was opened by the Archbishop of Canterbury in 1888.

The Attention to Detail

Octavia used to insist that her work depended on attention to detail, and that it was only by the unremitting concentration on seemingly tiny points that the work of reformation could be carried through. However, there was one detail, and it was quite a large one, concerning which she was very vague: she never knew exactly how many houses she was managing, or how many tenants she was responsible for. There is a rather comical section in her evidence to the Royal Commission on the Housing of the Working Classes in which the Commissioners made repeated attempts to get her to give the number of houses she managed, first to the nearest hundred, and then the nearest thousand, but without success.[18] Octavia said that she had never made the calculation, firstly because it would have served no purpose, and secondly because there were many helpers and ex-helpers managing property along 'Octavia Hill' lines, but without any formal ties to her.[19]

She was a bit more forthcoming with her fellow-workers. In her circular letter for 1874 Octavia said that she was managing fifteen blocks containing 2,000 - 3,000 tenants. Following the great expansion of her work in conjunction with the Ecclesiastical Commissioners in the 1890s and 1900s, Octavia was estimated to be controlling between 1,800 and 1,900 houses and flats, exclusive of rooms in tenements, by the time of her death in 1912.[20] Given the larger family size at that time, she must have been responsible for over 10,000 people. This sounds like a lot, and it was a lot for a woman who worked independently, and on no firmer basis than her own deeply-held convictions. However we need to remember that Octavia was not alone in her concern for the housing of the poor. Working-class housing, or social housing as we now call it, was one of the most active branches of Victorian philanthropy, and Octavia was joining a large and vigorous movement when she first walked into Paradise Place in 1864. In order to get her work into perspective we need to consider the other players.

Working-class Housing

There are certain strands of charitable activity which can be traced back for hundreds of years through the great histories of English philanthropy.[21] Education is the oldest. Almost from the time Henry VIII shut down the monasteries—which had been almost the sole providers of welfare services to the poor—public-spirited citizens endowed grammar schools to provide a ladder out of poverty for the children of the poor. Medical charities were prominent in the eighteenth century, which saw the foundation of five of the great London teaching hospitals between the 1720s and the 1740s.

The provision of housing to the poor as a charitable activity came later. With the exception of the rows of almshouses to accommodate a dozen of so worthy old people which adorned so many towns and villages, there was little philanthropic activity in the housing field before the nineteenth century. However, the Industrial Revolution was accompanied by significant population growth, and truly massive population displacement from country to town, which gave rise to slum housing conditions such as had never been seen before. Tens of thousands of working-class families were living in squalid, jerry-built tenements, often without any sort of plumbing or sanitation, and sometimes without the benefit of made-up roads and pavements. The sanitary reform movement, which was to prove so vitally important in addressing the related questions of slum housing and public health threats such as cholera, grew up in response to what was felt to be an intolerable situation.

In 1842 the Poor Law Commission published its *Report on the Sanitary Conditions of the Labouring Population and on the Means of its Improvement*. It had been written by Edwin Chadwick, Secretary to the Commission, who had used the channels of enquiry open to him through the Poor Law Commissioners to assemble an unprecedented mass of information on the insanitary living conditions of the poor. These resulted, according to Chadwick, in more deaths per year from preventable diseases than the battle of Waterloo. Chadwick's Report was one of the milestones along what was to be a very long road of nineteenth century legislative reform in the field of health and housing, but the work of reform was not to be entirely left to government. The provision of working-class housing, embodying the latest scientific knowledge of hygiene, became one of the greatest departments in the enterprise of Victorian philanthropy.

Even as Chadwick was assembling his statistics, private citizens were forming themselves into associations to tackle the problem. In 1844 Lord Ashley (later the seventh Earl of Shaftesbury), Dr Southwood Smith and others took over the old Labourer's Friend Society and re-launched it as the Society for Improving the Condition of the Labouring Classes (SICLC). The aim was to build model dwellings of different types to provide homes for the poor, but on a commercial basis. It was hoped that if it could be shown that it was possible to provide working-class housing along the latest sanitary lines and still make a profit, the market would take care of the slum problem. The dividend was limited to four per cent per year, and this was the beginning of the movement which came to be known as five per cent philanthropy, a peculiar Victorian solution to social problems which mixed business acumen with a social conscience. There were many societies which followed the SICLC, offering, in the words of The Metropolitan Association for Improving the Dwellings of the Industrious Classes, to provide the labouring man '...with an increase of the comforts and conveniences of life, with full compensation to the capitalist',[22] and some of them offered less than five per cent.[23] It was never likely that they would attract large numbers of serious investors on these terms, as almost any other form of investment would have produced a better rate of return. Commercial speculators building working-class tenements anticipated a ten per cent return on capital, as the houses were not expected to last for long. Any attempt to solve the slum problem on this basis, then, would require a lot of goodwill. As the *Builder* magazine put it, those intending to provide good quality housing for the poor would have to 'mix a little philanthropy with their per-centage calculations'.[24]

However, confident that investors could be tempted into the market if model schemes could be made to pay, the SICLC began with a street of cottages in Pentonville, followed by several lodging houses for men and boys. In 1849 it began its most important project, a development of Model Houses for Families in Streatham Street, near the British Museum. They were well in advance of the standards of their time, and when they were put on the market in 1850 at rents of between 4s and 7s a week, they proved very popular.[25]

Perhaps the Society's most famous effort was the construction of a set of model dwellings for artisans which were erected in Hyde Park for the Great Exhibition of 1851.[26] They proved to be a popular exhibit and were dismantled after the Exhibition to be re-erected at Kennington, where they still stand. The design was copied for other model building projects, both in this country and elsewhere. The SICLC did little more of significance after this. It had never intended to become a landlord on a large scale and, having created models for different types of working-class accommodation, it felt it had done its job.

The Metropolitan Association for Improving the Dwellings of the Industrious Classes was formed in 1841 and operated on a different scale. It intended to set itself up as a major provider of working-class housing, first of all in London and then throughout the country through its affiliated associations in Brighton, Newcastle, Dudley, Ramsgate, Southampton and elsewhere. Although promising investors a return of five per cent, this sank for several years to two per cent, with the result that its grander plans were never realised. Nevertheless, the Association was able to boast that, owing to its implementation of the latest knowledge of sanitation, the average rate of mortality in its buildings was less than one-third of that for London, while infant mortality was little more than a fifth.[27]

The 1860s saw the launch of several major new initiatives in social housing, as well as the start of Octavia Hill's work. In 1863 Sidney Waterlow, who had turned his family's stationery business into the great printing firm which still exists, formed the Improved Industrial Dwellings Company. It promised investors five per cent, and was able to meet this promise for many years. As a result it had no difficulty in attracting private capital, as well as being able to draw on cheap loans from the government under an Act of Parliament of 1866. The Company began with a block of model dwellings in Finsbury, but its largest venture was the Bethnal Green Estate, built in the early 1870s, to take advantage of the newly-opened Bethnal Green station, which made the area suitable for artisans' housing.

In 1867 the Artizans' Labourers' and General Dwellings Company was formed as a sort of building society, to enable working men to build and own their own homes. In the event most of its developments in London were still in the form of managed rented accommodation. They included large estates in Battersea (called Shaftesbury Park after the seventh Earl who was an active supporter), Kilburn and Noel Park.

The Peabody Donation Fund

However, all other developments in social housing were overshadowed by the launch, in 1862, of the Peabody Donation Fund, a body so generously endowed and so efficiently managed that it immediately became the most important player on the field—a position which, to a large extent, it still retains.

George Peabody was an American merchant and investment banker who spent most of his working life in London. He amassed a very great fortune and, being childless and unmarried, he devoted the last part of his life to giving vast quantities of it away. Towards the end of the 1850s he began to think about establishing a charitable body which would benefit the poor of London, the city to which he felt he owed so much. He went to speak to Lord Shaftesbury, the great philanthropist who by that time had almost acquired the status of a living saint, to talk to him about an educational fund. Education had always been Peabody's greatest interest, and indeed he is mainly remembered in his native country for the vast endowments which he made in that field. He seems to have been thinking about giving money to the Ragged Schools Union, of which Shaftesbury was the

President. Shaftesbury put him off this idea, partly because he felt that an organisation as *ad hoc* as the Ragged Schools Union would be fundamentally changed by the influx of a large amount of capital. Instead, he persuaded Peabody to think about the housing of the poor, in which Shaftesbury himself was becoming deeply involved at the time.

In 1862 Peabody announced the foundation of the Peabody Donation Fund, endowed by him with £150,000, with the aim of 'relieving the poor and needy of this great city, and to promote their comfort and happiness'. He did not specify that the Fund had to concern it self exclusively—or at all—with housing, but after considering other possibilities his Trustees decided to make this their special concern. In order to make the Fund self-perpetuating, whilst still a philanthropic venture, the Trustees decided to seek a return of three per cent on capital. Peabody's satisfaction with their actions was made evident in the further gifts of capital which he made to the Fund, amounting to £500,000 by the time of his death.

Peabody shared the concern, widespread amongst nineteenth century philanthropists, that the poor should only be helped in ways which encouraged independence and eventual self-sufficiency. As he told an audience in the Guildhall in 1866: 'The self-reliance and honest independence of the working people are the best guarantee of a country's prosperity and moral greatness'.[28] He had no intention of supporting the idle and feckless with his hard-earned money, and he made it a condition of his endowment of the Fund that:

> ...the sole qualification for participation in the benefits of the fund shall be an ascertained and continued condition of life such as brings the individual within the description (in the ordinary sense of the word) of 'the poor' of London; combined with moral character, and good conduct as a member of society.[29]

This is not, in fact a 'sole' qualification: it is two. The beneficiaries had to be poor *and* have a good character. It became normal practice to ask prospective tenants to produce an employer's reference, which excluded those in casual or irregular work. The Peabody Trustees were to be criticised over the years for doing nothing to help the very poorest—those below the level of the artisans—but they could defend themselves by saying that this had never been George Peabody's intention.[30] Indeed it was not the intention of any of those involved with philanthropic housing to work with this class of tenant—except Octavia. It was her unique claim to fame that she alone would take 'the tenants that nobody else will touch', because she was sure that by working closely with them, she could 'train' them to make them into the sort of model tenants with which the other associations started out.[31]

The first Peabody Buildings opened in Spitalfields in 1864, followed by Peabody Square in Islington in 1865. There were further estates in Chelsea, Bermondsey and Westminster which Peabody would have seen prior to his death in 1869. However the truly massive expansion of the Fund came in the decade which followed the passing of the 1875 Artisans' and Labourers' Dwellings Act, known as the Cross Act after the Home Secretary, R.A. Cross, who was responsible for it. This Act empowered the Metropolitan Board of Works to purchase (using compulsory powers if necessary) and to clear slum areas which had been deemed a public health threat. These cleared sites then had to be sold on to developers who would undertake to re-build them with working-class housing. There was an obligation to accommodate as many people as had been displaced, which was a strange condition since over-crowding had contributed to the original condemnation of the slums.[32]

Under these stringent conditions the Board of Works found it difficult to sell the sites at all. They had been valued under their compulsory purchase orders as if they had full commercial potential, but they were being sold on with severe limitations. By 1879 the Board was left with a series of large, vacant sites, and no bidders—except for the Peabody Donation Fund.

The Trustees offered about £120,000 for a group of sites,[33] which represented far less than the Board had paid for them.[34] As there was no one else with the sort of funds which the Peabody Trustees could command, coupled with the desire to build working-class housing on such a large scale, the Board had no option but to accept. What this meant was that the Peabody Estates which eventually covered the sites were heavily subsidised by the ratepayers, although there seems to have been an unwillingness to admit this on either side.[35]

In 1880 the Trustees took possession of the first site, in Whitechapel. This was followed by sites in Bedfordbury, Great Wild Street, Orchard Street, Whitecross Street, Clerkenwell and Hebrand Street. These were all large sites which were developed as Peabody Estates—not single blocks or groups of model dwellings which the other housing societies had been building. The sheer volume of units of accommodation provided was immense: by 1882 Peabody owned 3,500 dwellings housing more than 14,600 people,[36] and there were eight completely new estates between 1881 and 1885 alone.[37] However, even with George Peabody's enormous endowment fund, the Trustees had been obliged to borrow on a large scale to finance these projects. After 1885 they were obliged to pause to get their finances back in order, and in fact they built nothing more for twenty years. By that time the London County Council was busy building council estates, and private housing societies would never again take the lead in the field of social housing.

Local Authorities as Landlords

In the last part of the nineteenth century, the housing of the poor was a subject on which every educated person was expected to be informed, from the Queen and the Prince Consort down.[38] 'The attention of persons of every class, of every creed and school of politics, has been turned to this question', the Marquess of Salisbury told the House of Lords in 1884.[39] In the 1860s, when Octavia became actively involved, the spirit of *laissez-faire* still reigned, and any suggestion that the state should involve itself in the provision of housing, or any of the other 'necessary of life' (p. 94), was almost beyond serious consideration. This attitude was to change as the years went by, partly because the housing societies were perceived to be failing, in spite of their heroic efforts, as the population of London's poor was increasing faster than they could erect model dwellings.

The Royal Commission on the Housing of the Working Classes, which met in 1884, was partly provoked by the publication of a sensational pamphlet called *The Bitter Cry of Outcast London* in 1883. Published anonymously, it had been written by a Congregationalist minister called Andrew Mearns. He painted a lurid picture of the squalor in which parts of the working population were living, and called for 'state interference' in social issues such as housing. Octavia was rather contemptuous of *The Bitter Cry* and regarded it as propaganda for the 'prominent poor'— those idle and feckless people who make the most of their problems in the hope that someone else will bail them out (see p. 115). However, the pamphlet caused a stir and fed an already growing conviction that the government would have to intervene in the housing question in one way or another.

Octavia regarded such suggestions with horror. She believed that the working man should be able to pay for his own accommodation, and that subsidy of any kind would undermine his independence and effectively turn him into a second-class citizen. She told the Royal Commission that she hoped its findings would not result in anything which undermined the principle that 'homes should be self-supporting', and she warned them that:

> ...there is a sort of wild hope abroad amongst [the poor] and they have a sort of indefinite idea of the 'State' as having money independently of the collective body of taxpayers, and that things can be done without anybody paying for them.[40]

Her objections to what was called municipal housing came under four main headings (see pp. 94-95; 111-113; 116-117):

1. Local authorities would be able to use access to public funds to undercut the market, thus driving the private landlord out of business.

2. Public bodies are wasteful and extravagant, because they know they can cover themselves by raising tax levels. The prudent, working poor thus find themselves subsidising the feckless and the irresponsible.

3. Good management would become impossible because the tenants would also be their landlords' constituents. This would create a perverse incentive not to pursue arrears or to evict bad tenants, particularly if an election was in the offing.

4. To put local authorities in charge of projects involving major capital expenditure would be to invite corruption.

However, as the decade progressed, Octavia and those who shared her opposition to housing subsidies found that they were losing the argument. In 1888 the London County Council was created by Act of Parliament to replace the old Metropolitan Board of Works, and from the time it began to meet in 1889 the councillors made it clear that they intended to tackle the housing question by becoming landlords on a large scale. In December they met with the Secretary of State to demand the enlargement and clarification of the powers of local authorities to build and manage housing, and as a result of their lobbying the Housing of the Working Classes Act was passed in 1890, for which the Local Government Board had central government responsibility. This enabled local authorities to borrow money to buy land and build working-class housing. Such powers were not new: by a strange quirk, which seems to have passed almost unnoticed at the time, Lord Ashley, later the seventh Earl of Shaftesbury and a firm opponent of 'state benevolence', had put through parliament in 1851 the Labouring Classes Lodging Act which contained a clause enabling local authorities to borrow money or levy a rate to build houses. The powers were never invoked, and the 1851 Act itself was described as a dead letter by the Royal Commission in 1884,[41] but the London County Council, with its powers more clearly delineated under the 1890 Act, soon set to work.

After a couple of small schemes, the LCC started work in 1893 on the Boundary Street Estate, a fifteen-acre site in Shoreditch, which was given a completely new road layout and a series of blocks to accommodate 5,100 people. It was the first council estate, soon to be followed by the Millbank Estate (begun 1897), the Bourne Estate (begun 1900) and suburban estates in Tooting (begun 1899), Croydon (1901) and Tottenham (1912). The precedent set by the LCC was followed by other local authorities, slowly at first, but with increasing rapidity after the First World War. The supply of private working-class housing began to shrink, just as Octavia had predicted, as landlords found themselves undercut by public authorities. Then, in 1915, rent controls were introduced. The 1915 Rent and Mortgage Interest Act was a wartime measure, intended to last for the duration of the war and six months afterwards. Instead of that, it was confirmed by the 1919 Rent Act, and has never been lifted. Rent control, coupled with security of tenure legislation, has effectively choked the private rented sector. In 1914 88 per cent of all households were in the private rented sector;[42] by 1995 the figure was eight per cent[43]—and this includes private landlords who accept tenants whose rent is paid from housing benefit, who would otherwise be in bed and breakfast accommodation. In so far as it still exists as a source of housing for people who are paying their own way, the private rented sector caters for middle-class and professional tenants who can afford high rents and large deposits. Working-class housing in the sector has vanished (apart from the welfare cases), except for the housing associations which, as we shall see later, are now effectively divisions of the state sector. So, just as Octavia foretold (see p. 112), the

state entered working-class housing thinking it would supplement existing private provision, only to find itself left as virtually
the sole player. Working-class people now have less choice in
matters of housing than they had a hundred years ago.

Was There an Alternative?

Amongst social historians the Whiggish approach to history,
which sees everything as a natural progression towards an
inevitable end, is particularly strong. Philanthropy has therefore
come to be regarded as simply a necessary step on the way to
state welfare, as if no other sensible answer to social problems
could have been found.[44] Sometimes the philanthropists are
chided even for their successes, which put off the blissful advent
of state intervention. Even John Nelson Tarn, the author of the
excellent history of social housing *Five Per Cent Philanthropy*,
came to the conclusion that Octavia Hill 'had considerable
success on a limited scale, but her efforts were palliatives in
reality, and the day when the slums had to be demolished
because their environment was inadequate was only
postponed'.[45]

The trouble with this approach is that it projects backwards
into the past the intellectual fads and political prejudices of the
present. The problem is particularly acute in housing since most
modern commentators come from a left-wing political perspective
which assigns to the private landlord an especially low position
in its demonology. Anything which leads to the destruction of
landlordism, therefore, registers as 'a good thing'. The result, as
M.J. Daunton points out in his book *A Property-Owning Democracy?* is that: '[m]uch historical work on housing is consequently
more indicative of the policy consensus of the 1960s than of the
past'.[46]

Those who see council housing as the only solution to the
problem of housing the poor like to make much of the supposedly
hopeless inadequacy of the charitable bodies, faced with an
escalating social problem which must outstrip their resources.
However, this analysis ignores the scope of the housing societies,
which was already immense by the end of the nineteenth
century. By 1895 the Peabody Trust had built about 5,100
dwellings, the Improved Industrial Dwellings Company 5,350 and
the Artizans' Labourers' and General Dwellings Company nearly
6,500,[47] and these were just the largest groups in a very wide-

spread movement. There were hundreds of other associations, some small ones formed by local people to erect a few badly-needed blocks in their own towns, others endowed by wealthy people like Angela Burdett-Coutts, that *grande dame* of Victorian philanthropy, who built Columbia Square in Bethnal Green entirely at her own expense. There were also the industrialists who were developing important schemes to house their work-forces in complete model communities, like Cadbury (Bournville), Rowntree (New Earswick) and Lever (Port Sunlight). When the opportunity presented itself the societies could work together on large-scale redevelopments, like the Whitechapel Improvement Scheme, begun in 1875, which involved the Peabody Trustees, Canon Barnett's East End Dwellings Company and the Roths-childs' 4% Industrial Dwellings Company.[48] The philanthropic movement to provide working-class housing did not expire from its own inadequacy: it was cut off in its prime by public policy.

It was by no means inevitable that the housing of the poor should be taken out of the hands of private landlords and philanthropic societies. It *was* inevitable, as Octavia pointed out (p. 112), that, once local authorities began to provide housing, their access to public money would allow them to force the other players off the pitch, so that they would become effectively the *only* providers of social housing.

Octavia and the Environment

One of Oscar Wilde's characters says that she has attended a lecture on 'the influence of morals on fabrics, or fabrics on morals, I forget which'. This is a *reductio ad absurdum* of a serious debate which was taking place throughout the last half of the nineteenth century on what we would call environmental factors: does a good environment improve people's behaviour, or do they have to better themselves before they can appreciate a good environment?[49]

This was a question of vital importance to those involved with the housing of the poor. The advocates of state aid argued that it would make sense for the government to provide good housing as it would reduce crime; Octavia argued that it made no sense to put her 'destructive class' of tenants into model dwellings equipped with every modern appliance, which they would soon vandalise and turn into another slum. Samuel Morley MP, hosiery tycoon and philanthropist, put it in a nutshell:

> Many people begin at the wrong end. They say people drink because they live in bad dwellings; I say they live in bad dwellings because they drink. It makes all the difference the way you put it. The first essential is not to deal with the habitation, but the habit.[50]

However the matter was by no means as simple as Morley suggested, and we sometimes find people arguing on both sides of the question. Octavia herself was not quite as definite on the issue as she sometimes made out, as the Royal Commissioners found when they tried to pin her down:

> Q. You said... that you found that under these improved circumstances the people get very much better in their manners and habits?
>
> A. Yes.
>
> Q. Then might we draw this deduction that it is the circumstances in which they live that make these people bad?
>
> A. I cannot say that it is the circumstances wholly. You find beautiful exceptions amongst people in just the same circumstances. It is the men and the circumstances together; you cannot say which it is.[51]

However, while Octavia never wavered in her view that spanking new blocks of model dwellings would not, in themselves, re-moralise the lowest class of tenants which she dealt with, she had no reservations about the beneficial effects of the environment in the larger sense—the garden, the common land, the fine landscape. 'The poor of London need joy and beauty in their lives' (p. 56). From the time she first started working with her young charges in the Ladies' Guild she liked to organise outings to the countryside for the poor. For Octavia, who had enjoyed a blissfully happy childhood in the countryside which then constituted Finchley and Highgate, country air and fine views were an unmitigated force for good. The happiness which she felt she was able to give the tenants of Freshwater Place in Marylebone when she laid out the little playground (pp. 55-56) led to a life-long involvement with the campaign to preserve open spaces. First of all it was the small patch of land in the town centre—especially graveyards and burial grounds—which could provide an 'open-air sitting room' for the poor. This led to larger scale campaigns, mainly conducted through the Open Spaces sub-committee of the Kyrle Society, set up by Octavia's sister Miranda for 'the diffusion of beauty' in 1876. The chairman of this sub-committee was Robert Hunter, whom Octavia had met through the Commons Preservation Society, of which he was

Honorary Solicitor. The first of Octavia's major preservation campaigns was to save Swiss Cottage Fields, where she had played as a child, from development. This was unsuccessful since, in August 1875, when Octavia had already raised £8,150 out of the £10,000 purchase price, the owners withdrew their offer and built Fitzjohn's Avenue on the site. Octavia had greater success with the campaign to save Parliament Hill Fields in 1886, and there was an increasing number of smaller victories following the passage of the 1881 Metropolitan Open Spaces Act which made it easier to transfer gardens and graveyards to local authorities. However, Octavia and Robert Hunter both realised that one major obstacle to the preservation of the countryside was the lack of any institution capable of accepting and managing large tracts of land. The Kyrle Society and the Commons Preservation Society were both small bodies, with neither the personnel nor the funds to act as property managers. It became clear that a new body was needed which could undertake land management on a large scale on behalf of the nation. They were supported in this by Canon Rawnsley, who had as a young curate in Soho been one of Octavia's housing managers in Drury Lane, but who had retreated to the more congenial surroundings of the Lake District. Octavia and Robert Hunter had both supported him in his efforts to preserve the beauty of the landscape there, and together they were responsible for forming what Octavia originally intended to call The Commons and Gardens Trust. When she wrote to Hunter suggesting the name he scribbled across the top of the letter '?National Trust. RH'.

The National Trust was formally constituted in 1895, and has been so extraordinarily successful ever since that many people have a vague idea that it is part of the government. In fact, it is very much a part of civil society.[52] It has 2.4 million members and regularly comes at the top of the list of fundraising charities in Britain.[53] It is the largest private landowner in the country,[54] owning 1.43 per cent of the total land area of England, Wales and Northern Ireland and protecting 18 per cent of the coastline, as well as hundreds of historic properties.[55] It represents Octavia Hill's most lasting contribution to the British way of life. Unfortunately its immense scale, which Octavia could never have foreseen, now overshadows her other work to the point at which anything else she did is seen as irrelevant or as simply a stepping-stone to the foundation of this great institution.

Work Among the Poor

However, for Octavia, her work in the open spaces movement was not distinct from her housing work: they went together. She called them 'two developments of the same object, for to us in London, no less than to the dweller in the country, the house and the garden together form the home. We in London have to share our garden, perhaps England itself will learn to share some of its gardens'.[56] She saw no essential difference between opening up city-centre graveyards as 'open-air sitting rooms for the poor', and preserving a hilltop in Kent for everyone to enjoy. More importantly, however, Octavia's open spaces campaigning, like her housing work and everything else she did, grew out of her over-riding concern for the poor. This seems strange to us, now that National Trust membership has become a middle-class badge of belonging, and the Trust seems to have mislaid Octavia's concern for the poor somewhere beneath its acorn-sprigged stationery and bags of potpourri, but Octavia's Letters to Fellow-Workers were all described on their title-pages as an 'account of donations received for work among the poor'. This covered everything, from saving Parliament Hill Fields to organising flower shows in the Red Cross Hall in Southwark. From her early teens, when her father's departure from the household had thrust her into a premature adulthood, everything she did was motivated by a passionate concern for the condition of the poor.

This concern was matched by an equally strong conviction that, whilst the rich were morally obliged to help the poor, there was a further serious obligation to do this in a way which would build up the character of those being helped and set them on the road to independence. She was horrified by the thought of handouts to idlers. 'There are two main principles to be observed in any plan for raising the poorest class in England', she told the Social Science Association in Bristol in 1869. 'One is that personal influence must be brought strongly to bear on the individuals. The other that the rich must abstain from any form of almsgiving.'[57]

In the same year Octavia became a founder member of the Society for Organising Charitable Relief and Repressing Mendicity, which soon became known as the Charity Organisation Society (COS). COS was not intended to be an agency for distribution of welfare services, but rather a referral agency, liaising between the local Poor Law guardians and charities. The intention was to thoroughly investigate any applicant for assistance to see if the circumstances were genuine, if there was really no other source of help available, and to decide on the best method of assisting without demoralising the recipient with doles. The system was extremely complicated and was never fully put into effect except in Octavia's own parish of St Mary's, Bryanston Square, and even there it did not long survive her departure after personality clashes on the committee.

The hardline COS approach regarded state doles as anathema, and Octavia opposed all attempts to create rights-based state welfare services throughout her lifetime. Although COS was strongly criticised throughout its existence for being hard-hearted, this was not a charge which was likely to stick in Octavia's case. Her concern for the poor was transparently genuine, and her housing work, which was run on absolutely orthodox COS lines, was having a very obvious good effect on her tenants.

The Commission on the Poor Law

Octavia's status as an authority on all matters pertaining to the poor was such that, in 1905, she was asked to become a member of the Royal Commission on the Poor Law.[58] The Poor Law, last revised in 1834, was generally regarded as incapable of meeting the needs of an advanced industrial economy. Reform was inevitable, but what form was it to take? Octavia found amongst her fellow commissioners a number of old friends and colleagues like Charles Booth, C.S. Loch, Helen Bosanquet and Beatrice Webb. With at least six strong proponents of the COS line among the Commissioners,[59] it was reasonable to assume that the Commission would not come out in favour of a social welfare state along Bismarckian lines.

The Commissioners met between 1905 and 1909. Their work was arduous and time-consuming, involving much travelling around the country to collect evidence, and Octavia had to re-arrange her commitments to do the work properly. When the Majority Report was published it contained a number of recommendations for improving the workings of the Poor Law which, although modest enough, still caused Octavia to enter her own memorandum of dissent. She objected to recommendations for free medical treatment for the poor, and to the idea that the government should create jobs during times of recession.

However the Minority Report, signed by Beatrice Webb but in reality largely written by her husband Sidney, was far more radical. This called for the abolition of the Poor Law system and its administration through Boards of Guardians altogether and for the transfer of its responsibilities to local authority-run bodies dealing with particular areas such as education and health. The Minority Report also called for labour exchanges and unemployment benefit.

Of course, it was the Minority Report which indicated the way ahead for welfare provision. The Royal Commission represented a sort of Indian summer for the COS viewpoint. Octavia was nearing the end of her life and—unfortunately perhaps—lived just long enough to see the passage of Acts of Parliament which introduced the things she had fought most bitterly against, like state pensions, which she was sure would undermine thrift and self-reliance.

The Legacy

On 1 December 1898 Octavia was invited to attend a gathering of her closest friends at Grosvenor House, the Duke of Westminster's London home in Park Lane. The occasion was to mark her sixtieth birthday, and her friends presented her with her own portrait, painted by the leading portrait artist of the day, John Singer Sargent. The occasion was obviously an emotional one for Octavia and, although she still had fourteen years to live and much work still ahead of her, her speech of acceptance made it clear that her thoughts were inclining towards her own demise:

> When I am gone, I hope my friends will not try to carry out any special system, or to follow blindly in the track which I have trodden. New circumstances require various efforts, and it is the spirit, not the dead form that should be perpetuated. When the time comes that we slip from our places, and they are called to the front as workers, what should they inherit from us? Not a system, not an association, not dead formulas. We shall leave them a few houses, purified and improved, a few new and better ones built, a certain record of thoughtful and loving management, a few open spaces, some of which will be more beautiful than they would have been, but what we care most to leave them is not any tangible thing, however great, not any memory, however good, but the quick eye to see, the true soul to measure, the large hope to grasp the mighty issues of the new and better days to come—greater ideals, greater hope and patience to realise both.[60]

Octavia's persistent refusal to form any sort of association (pp. 87 and 119) made problems for her fellow-workers when she eventually died in 1912. These women found themselves trying to keep alive the principles of the Octavia Hill system of housing management in an increasingly hostile environment, with local authority housing posing an ever greater threat to the survival of the philanthropic bodies. Not unnaturally, they decided to ignore Octavia's wishes and form themselves into an association for mutual support.

In 1916 the Association of Women Housing Workers was formed, consisting of women who had worked with Octavia at some time. It almost immediately renamed itself the Association of Women Housing Property Managers. At about the same time another organisation, the Octavia Hill Club, was formed by Miss Jeffrey, who had been Octavia's secretary and was managing the Crown Commissioners' Cumberland Market estate. Inevitably there was rivalry between the two, which was resolved when they merged in 1932 to become the Society of Women Housing Estate Managers (SWHEM). The aim of the Society was to promote the involvement of women in housing management along Octavia Hill lines. It insisted on thorough training and professional status. It negotiated terms of employment for its members and resisted attempts to relegate women to the 'social work' side of housing management, while men were given the important positions.

For by now the situation had changed fundamentally. The involvement of local authorities in housing, slow at first, had entered a new era with the passing of the 1919 Housing and Town Planning Act, known as the Addison Act, which imposed upon local authorities the duty of surveying the housing needs of their areas and submitting plans to meet them. Local authorities were to become landlords, whether they wanted to or not.

As local authority housing departments grew, it became obvious that housing management was a 'proper' job—the sort of job men could do without feeling embarrassed about it. As municipal housing was displacing all other participants in the field of social housing, members of SWHEM found themselves with little option but to forget about Octavia's objections and go to work for the local authorities. By 1936 the Society had 143 qualified members, 62 of whom worked for local authorities.[61] However they found themselves competing with an ever-growing contingent of men, some of whom were inclined to point out to them that their proper place was in the home and not taking jobs from heads of families.[62]

These men were represented by the Institute of Housing, formed in 1931, of which the membership was almost exclusively male and drawn from the public sector. There were originally some women from SWHEM who belonged to IOH as well, but as hostility towards women in general and the SWHEM in particular became explicit in IOH publications it was decided in 1936 that SWHEM members should resign *en masse* from IOH. The women had a fairly low opinion of IOH members in any case, as the organisation had no entrance qualifications and no training programme. SWHEM was, in fact, still the only body to be offering training in housing management.

Nevertheless, there were women who felt that their training programmes should be open to men, otherwise the calibre of housing managers working in local authority housing was not likely to rise. A motion to this effect was put to the AGM in 1943 and passed. In her excellent history of *Women in the Housing Service* (from which most of this account is taken) Marion Brion quotes one of the women who was on the original committee of SWHEM set up to consider the proposal:

> I can remember Miss Samuel pleading, with tears in her eyes, 'If you let men in, they'll take over all the best jobs, they'll be the Directors of Housing, you'll be the rent collectors'.[63]

This proved to be sadly prophetic. In 1949 it was decided to admit men as full members of the Society, and in 1965, after years of agitation and discussion between the two bodies, SWHEM and IOH merged to become the Institute of Housing Managers. It soon became clear that, just as some of the women had warned, this was not a merger but a takeover. In order to protect the women's identity it had been written into the original agreement that the Council of the new body should represent that of the two old bodies for three years—seven women to fifteen men. As soon as the three-year-period was up the women were dropped from the relevant committees, and found that all traces of the old SWHEM were being removed. Noticeboards erected in the main rooms of the Institute's offices gave presidents of the IOH from 1931 to 1965, then presidents of the joint body, but no reference was made to SWHEM.[64] The name was changed back to Institute of Housing in 1975, which was regarded by the

women as having symbolic significance, and the spirit of Octavia
Hill became more and more difficult to detect in social housing
management.

Building Utopia

When Octavia was writing her Letter to Fellow-Workers for the
year of 1911 she was dying of cancer, and must have realised
that she would not write another. It was clearly intended as a
farewell:

> As I write to record what has been done, a song of thankfulness seems
> to be singing in my heart as I think of the many and great mercies
> which have been with us, of the joy which has been sent to us, and of
> how day by day strength has been given to follow the way, and light
> to see it, not far ahead, but sufficient for daily guidance.

Alas, Octavia's acceptance of the limited perspective of the day-
by-day approach did not appeal to the new breed of (male)
municipal housing managers. The friction between the men and
the women in housing management did not stem entirely from
sexist notions about a woman's place being in the home. It owed
just as much to their fundamental differences in approach to the
issue. The women, following Octavia's system, were interested in
small-scale, detailed work with individual tenants. The men
wanted to use social housing to build Utopia.[65]

Le Corbusier's vision of the city of towers proved intoxicating
to those planners who felt that a comprehensive programme of
state welfare, including housing, would not only eliminate forever
such social horrors as slum housing, but would also create better
people living in a better society. The construction of social
housing, which took on new dimensions in the years after the
Second World War, entered a new phase with the introduction of
system building in the 1960s. Suddenly it seemed possible to
create accommodation, cheaply and by the thousands of units,
which would see the whole nation happily housed in model
communities.

The contrast between the planners' rhetoric and the reality of
living on those estates was so great that it is difficult for us now
to believe that anyone could seriously have thought that the idea
would work. Firstly, system building proved to have such fatal
flaws, notably the admission of damp through joints in the
concrete sections, that many of the buildings deteriorated within

a few years to the point at which it became more sensible to demolish them than to try to repair them. This was in spite of the fact that the local authorities concerned will be paying interest on the loans they took out to build them until well into the next century. Secondly, the social problems which have dogged these estates have been of such a different order to anything which had been seen before in this country that, were the philanthropists of the nineteenth century able to visit Easterhouse and Meadow Well today, they would wonder if they were in Britain.

Octavia had warned that, if social housing projects became too large—and she considered some of the Peabody Estates to be too large—then the tenants would become unmanageable as they would no longer be treated as individuals with their own needs and circumstances. She warned that staircases and common areas would become the haunts of roughs (pp. 106-7) who would terrorise the law-abiding residents. But she could never have imagined the ghastliness of late twentieth-century inner-city estates, covering hundreds of acres, in which the breakdown of the social order is so complete that the rule of law could scarcely be said to apply. She could never have imagined parts of England in which the tradition of consensual policing would become impossible and in which policemen would regularly need to be armed, in which drug dealing and other criminal activities would form the normal way of life for large numbers of people, and in which attempts to enforce the law could result in rioting, looting and murder. We are inclined to feel superior when we read accounts of Victorian slums, with their earth floors, lack of drainage and windowless rooms. How could such a state of affairs have been tolerated by a civilised nation? But the brutality and hardened criminality of life on our inner-city sink estates had no counterpart in Victorian England.

The Housing Association Movement

As M.J. Daunton points out in his book *A Property-Owning Democracy?*, it would be difficult to think of any other sector of the economy which has been so thoroughly manipulated by state intervention as housing. Increasing control of the rented sector through successive rent acts, coupled with ever-greater subsidies to council housing, have effectively wiped out private-sector rented housing for the working classes. At the same time, generous tax concessions to owner occupiers have pushed all who could afford it—including many low-earners—into becoming mortgagees.[66]

The private rented sector has thus been squeezed from both sides. Those at the upper end have moved into owner-occupation, while those at the lower end have had no choice but to become tenants of their local authority. However there is still a remnant of the great Victorian movement to provide housing for those on low incomes on a philanthropic basis. It is represented by the housing associations, and it is in the housing association movement that we would expect to find the continuing tradition of working-class housing provision on a basis which is neither state-run nor commercial in its orientation. Unfortunately this expectation would be disappointed.

Like other areas of the voluntary sector, the housing association movement has now been thoroughly colonised by the state. There is, of course, a big question mark over just how 'voluntary' the voluntary sector really is, when so many of its component bodies are receiving 50 per cent or more of their incomes from the state.[67] However, the element of subsidy is not spread evenly around the sector. Out of more than £3.4 billion given by central government to the 'voluntary' sector in 1994-5, £2.07 billion, or 60 per cent of the total, was accounted for by a single grant from the Department of the Environment to the Housing Corporation.[68] The Housing Corporation then apportions this between more than 2,200 housing associations or 'registered social landlords' (RSLs) which it 'funds and promotes, registers and supervises'.[69] Most of this money goes to cover the capital costs of new housing.

The Corporation was set up under the Labour government of 1964-6 'to fill the gap between the shrinking private rental market and the dominant local authority sector'.[70] The emphasis in the early years was on building new houses for 'fair rent' and the development of co-ownership schemes.[71] The great period of expansion began with the 1974 Housing Act which introduced a capital subsidy to registered housing associations of up to 100 per cent, known as Housing Association Grant.[72] This was accompanied by Revenue Deficit Grant to bridge the gap between rents (which were ever-more strictly controlled) and costs which were rising because of inflation.

The situation changed again with the 1988 Housing Act which ended the 100 per cent subsidies and sought a mixture of public and private finance to meet capital costs. The percentage of subsidy available to meet the capital costs of each new house was reduced, and associations were encouraged to bridge the gap with loans from banks and building societies. Rent controls were withdrawn and consequently the Revenue Deficit Grant was scrapped, to be replaced by a mechanism called the Grant Redemption Fund, through which the government sought to claw back any surplus which arose if rents collected exceeded costs.

According to the Housing Corporation, the aim of the 1988 Act was to turn housing associations into 'major providers of new social housing in England, taking over from local authorities'.[73] Whilst this may have been technically accurate, it is difficult to see in what sense the housing associations could be expected to 'take over' housing provision from their local authorities when their independence had already been severely compromised by more than two decades of state funding, during which they had become so closely tied-in to their local authority housing departments that one critic has described them as in danger of becoming 'little more than the government's estate agent'.[74]

Like other charities which have been drawn into the 'contract culture', housing associations have found that public money brings with it a measure of political control. Housing associations which are in receipt of grants are expected to take a percentage of referrals from the local authority as a *quid pro quo*.[75] According to the Audit Commission about 60 per cent of housing associations' new tenants (excluding transfers) are nominated by local authorities.[76]

The Octavia Hill Housing Trust is the direct descendant of the Horace Street Trust which was set up by Octavia in 1888 to hold some properties which had been given to her by their owners. After her death it merged with other housing trusts, adopting its present name in 1991. It now owns about 1,400 properties and manages about 500 more on behalf of their owners. It received just over £1 million from the Housing Corporation in 1996/7, mostly for new building projects, and government subsidy accounted for over 40 per cent of its total turnover.[77] In return, the Trust is expected to take a percentage of nominations—approximately 75 per cent—from the housing department of the Royal Borough of Kensington and Chelsea. The remainder of its stock is kept either for rehousing its existing tenants or for referrals from agencies such as local charities working with the homeless or disabled. The Octavia Hill Housing Trust is currently participating in a pilot scheme called the Common Computerised Housing Register, giving it direct access to the local authority's housing database which includes everyone in line for social housing, whatever their current situation. In fact, the Trust has not maintained its own waiting list for over ten years. Thus, if a two-bedroomed flat becomes vacant, and it represents part of the stock allocated for local authority nomination, the database is consulted to find out who is at the top of the list for such a property. An applicant's position on the list is determined by 'housing need', which in turn is determined by a points system based on a number of indicators. It is important to remember that housing need is a political construct: it reflects a combination of the local authority's priorities combined with their statutory responsibilities laid down by parliament. In reality, this means that any unit which becomes available will, in all probability, go to a homeless person or family, usually a lone parent with dependent children.

It is now beginning to be recognised as a problem within the housing sector that such an approach to allocating housing (whether by housing association or local authority) results in a high concentration of multiple-needs households, which in turn soon leads to the creation of sink estates with unmanageable social problems. A study from the Joseph Rowntree Foundation identifies new entrants into the social housing sector as being different from households in both the private rented sector and owner-occupation in that they are more likely to be lone parents and to be economically inactive. '[T]he social and economic base of the sector is becoming ever narrower... These trends make it harder to sustain stable communities'.[78]

Lone parents and the homeless clearly have housing needs which should be met, but it is open to question whether they are best met by herding them together like this. Octavia's approach was very different:

> Our success depends on duly arranging the inmates; not too many children in any one house, so as to overcrowd it; not too few, so as to overcrowd another; not two bad people side by side, or they drink

together; not a terribly bad person beside a very respectable one (p. 74).

But Octavia's approach would not be acceptable now, because it was based on intuition and discretion, not on a points-based system of housing need.

That is not the only respect in which Octavia would find the modern housing association movement unrecognisable. Octavia believed passionately that 'a working man ought to be able to pay for his own house' (p. 44). She had a horror of having to depend on others for support, and she thought highly enough of her working-class tenants to believe that they would share her feelings. It was partly because of her abhorrence of subsidies and handouts, either by profligate charities or by state agencies, that she kept separate sets of books for every property or group of properties she managed, and she insisted that her housing managers had to balance their books to the last halfpenny every week. She felt that it was vitally necessary to be able to pay five per cent on the capital after clearing all other charges. Her tenants were thus fully-functioning members of society, not second-class citizens needing handouts.

The situation is very different today. As we have already mentioned, the state is putting over two billion pounds a year into the housing associations through the Housing Corporation, but that does not represent the end of the element of subsidy. According to the Audit Commission, about two-thirds of the housing associations' rental income is paid for through housing benefit.[79] So, even when properties have been built and managed with access to public funds, large numbers of tenants are still not paying the artificially low rents which are being charged! The situation in local authority housing is far worse, owing to the debt problem. Not only are local authorities using public money to build their estates, and then charging subsidised rents which are often paid out of the social security budget: in many cases they are not even able to collect the rents on these easiest of easy terms. It is not unusual for inner-city authorities to measure their rent arrears in millions of pounds—and in tens of millions in some of the more notorious cases. It is not just the case that social housing is now heavily subsidised. Owing to the mesh of grants, benefits and bad debts, we really cannot say how large the subsidy is.

Lessons for Today

The first full-length biography of Octavia Hill did not appear until 1942. It was written by Enid Moberly Bell with the permission and co-operation of the surviving relatives. Whilst there are certain disadvantages to such 'official' biographies—notably the danger that unflattering material may be suppressed—there is also the advantage that the biographer has access to those who knew and worked with the subject, and can give accounts of hopes, fears and beliefs from personal experience. Perhaps because of this, Enid Moberly Bell's empathy with her subject is such that, at times, it could almost be Octavia's words we are reading. The book concludes with some speculation on what solutions Octavia would have proposed to the 'vast problems we shall be called upon to face in the near future' (i.e. after the end of the Second World War):

> [T]hat every individual has a contribution to make to the common life and is immeasurably the poorer if he is not enabled to make it, and that therefore the only cure of the ills of society lies in the conversion and education of individual men and women—these things it may safely be affirmed she would assert today. It may be that the brave new world will be built on foundations other than hers, but it can hardly be doubted that in the process of rebuilding there will be need of the shrewd judgement, the self-forgetting devotion, and above all the invincible faith in righteousness that Octavia Hill brought to the task of her generation.[80]

It is perhaps superfluous to observe that the brave new post-war world was indeed built on foundations other than Octavia's. The series of acts of parliament which created the rights-based, cradle-to-grave, welfare state we know today violated Octavia's most deeply-held principles. Octavia had described the public provision to the working classes of any 'necessary of life' like housing as a 'disastrous policy' (p. 94). The welfare state provided not only housing, but health care, unemployment benefit, pensions, education and every conceivable 'necessary of life', 'free at the point of delivery', not only to the poor but—even more strangely, Octavia would have thought—to the rich as well.

It is because Octavia maintained the sternest line against any form of subsidy or state provision to the end of her life—to the exasperation of colleagues like Beatrice Webb and the Barnetts, who felt that she was failing to read the signs of the times—that she has come in for so much unfavourable comment in the last part of the twentieth century. Social policy analysts, who tend to come from the political left, have either ignored her completely or heaped abuse on her head. According to one:

> [T]he legacy she left to housing managers has been baneful. She founded a tradition which is inconsistent with the rights of tenants and destructive of their welfare.[81]

Even David Owen, in his magisterial history of English philanthropy, can scarcely conceal his exasperation with 'the inexorably moralistic individualism of Octavia Hill':

> Though her contemporaries regarded her as an oracle on working-class housing and her accomplishments in the field were, in fact, staggering they no longer command unquestioning admiration... they were... expressions of a social outlook that today is almost incomprehensible.[82]

Clearly there is more going on here than resentment at Octavia's hostility to state action. Other Victorian philanthropists who opposed state intervention, like Lord Shaftesbury, have not been so savagely dealt with. The vilification of Octavia has just as much to do with another characteristic which is even more likely to stick in the throat of the modern social-policy intellectual: her insistence on the moral dimension of welfare work.

Octavia believed that any assistance given to the poor had an inescapable moral component: it could either be given in a way which built them up and encouraged self-help and independence, or in a way which led to pauperism, or what we would call welfare dependency. Octavia was not alone in this belief: indeed it has been described by Gertrude Himmelfarb as 'the common denominator that linked together public relief and private charity, settlement houses and housing projects, socialist organizations and temperance societies'.[83] However Octavia emphasised the moral dimension more than most, because she was working with people who were at the bottom of the heap, and who were regarded as being beyond help by the other philanthropic housing societies. Octavia insisted that these people could not be helped by any amount of money spent on new properties, because their problems were as much internal as external:

> [T]he problem before you is far more difficult than the financial one; ...it is more complicated than that of building; ...you will have, before you can raise these very poorest, to help them to become better in themselves (p. 103).

There is never any shortage of visionaries who believe that poverty can be eliminated if only we will spend enough money. Octavia's hard-headed realism brings such fantasies down to earth with a bump. Furthermore, she insisted that no Acts of Parliament, no system of relief, no elaborate structures of inspection and regulation, and no new discipline of statistics, could ever help the poor *of themselves*. What was necessary was for educated, prosperous and dedicated people to work patiently, on a one-to-one basis, with individual poor people and their multiple problems. This sounded like hard work a hundred years ago and it still sounds like hard work now.

Of course, the talk of 'bettering' the poor has exposed Octavia to every criticism in the lexicon of political correctness. She is said to have been patronising, controlling, unbending and—most abhorred of all—judgmental. She would have agreed with 'judgmental'; indeed she would have been amazed that anyone could have considered the word pejorative. Of course she was judgmental; she had to use her judgement in hundreds of small matters every day of her working life, trying to help people who had enjoyed few advantages in life to do the best for themselves. As she told her helpers:

> [Y]our subtlest work is by no means ameliorating the outward condition of your people, but making them better, and ...you will do this by helping their weak wills to do what they know to be right (p. 120).

If Octavia had set out deliberately to write a sentence which would enrage the Dave Spart stereotype of the social worker/ social-policy academic, she could have done no better than this, but perhaps it is now Dave Spart, and not Octavia, who is out of date.

The most interesting aspect of the current debate on welfare reform is the introduction of the moral dimension. We now know that money is not enough to redress the problems of the really poor. Higher expenditure on welfare has not brought about a reduction in social problems. If there is any correlation, it seems to be working in the other direction. Policy analysts from Charles Murray[84] to Frank Field[85] have been pointing out that the rigidity of state welfare has an inescapable tendency to reward the sort of behaviour which we should be discouraging, and to penalise the sort of behaviour which we should be encouraging. Murray's identification of an 'underclass', defined by a type of poverty rather than a degree of poverty, has entered the mainstream of academic debate. Underclass status is characterised by anti-social attitudes in childbearing, by a lack of participation in the workforce, and by a lifestyle funded by a combination of welfare benefits and crime. These are all moral problems which we cannot spend our way out of, however much we might wish to do so. They need to be addressed on a moral plane by people whose convictions about the rightness and wrongness of certain types of behaviour are not forever in a state of flux. But where will we find such people now? Who now would respond to Octavia's appeal?

> The sense of the solemnity of life and its high responsibility is increasing among men, and the form it is taking is that of desiring to serve the poor. The same spirit which prompted men in another age to free the Holy Land, to found monasteries, to enter our own Church, now bids them work for men as men; for the poor first, as having nothing but their manhood to commend them to notice (p. 82).

It all sounds faintly ridiculous, because it is so long since anyone spoke of work among the poor in this way, but that is our loss. David Owen's attack on Octavia (p. 36) was published in 1965, when enthusiasm for the welfare state was still at a high level. In a strange way Octavia's 'social outlook' is less 'incomprehensible' to us now than the Utopian views of the architects and advocates of the welfare state.

Octavia as an Author

Octavia wrote very little for publication. Her two books, *The Homes of the London Poor* (1875) and *Our Common Land* (1877), were slim collections of previously published articles.[86] There were a few more articles which did not appear in book form, but, apart from letters to the newspapers, nothing else. Her *Letters to Fellow-Workers*, which gave accounts of the work to her supporters on an almost annual basis from 1872 to 1911, were printed for private circulation only. Octavia resisted all attempts to persuade her to publish them as she said she would not be able to speak so frankly of her hopes—and her failures—if they were addressed to the general public.

Given her limited output it is remarkable that she wrote so well. She was able to be, at the same time, both practical and idealistic, discussing drainage in the same paragraph as God's love of his creation (p. 110) and housing management in terms of bringing souls to Christ (p. 80). She managed to be factual without being coarse and visionary without being absurd: that was the strength of her writing, and one of the sources of the great influence which she exerted over her followers and supporters.

The essays and letters which follow are taken from a variety of sources. The first three chapters come from *The Homes of the London Poor*. Chapter Four contains extracts from the Letters to Fellow-Workers, which have never been published in their entirety. Chapters Five and Nine are taken from magazine articles which were not re-published in book-form. Chapter Six is Octavia's contribution to Charles Booth's great survey *Life and Labour of the People in London*. Chapter Seven began life as a letter to the editor of *The Times*, and Chapter Eight is taken from the manuscript text of Octavia's address to the Edinburgh Social Union in 1902, which has never been published before. These pieces have all been selected because they illustrate Octavia's views on housing, and as such they give only a partial view of her wide field of interests. The argument about open spaces was won so long ago that it scarcely seems worth going over again, but other aspects of Octavia's concern for the lives of the poor have had to be excluded on grounds of space. For ease of reference the chapters have been printed in date order but, as far as content is concerned, it would have made no difference if they had been in the reverse order. Octavia formed her views early in life and never saw the need to change them in any fundamental way.

It is extraordinary to reflect that Octavia's books have been out of print and her writings virtually unavailable throughout the twentieth century except for a few short collections of extracts.[87] The present collection is being published by the IEA Health and Welfare Unit in the belief that Octavia's views on social housing have an important contribution to make to the contemporary debate.

*Essays and Letters by
Octavia Hill*

Cottage Property in London

───────────────────────────────────────

*T*HE subject of dwellings for the poor is attracting so much attention, that an account of a small attempt to improve them may be interesting to many readers, especially as the plan adopted is one which has answered pecuniarily, and which, while it might be undertaken by private individuals without much risk, would bring them into close and healthy communication with their hard-working neighbours.

Two years ago I first had an opportunity of carrying out the plan I had long contemplated, that of obtaining possession of houses to be let in weekly tenements to the poor. That the spiritual elevation of a large class depended to a considerable extent on sanitary reform was, I considered, proved; but I was equally certain that sanitary improvement itself depended upon educational work among grown-up people; that they must be urged to rouse themselves from the lethargy and indolent habits into which they have fallen, and freed from all that hinders them from doing so. I further believed that any lady who would help to obtain things, the need of which they felt themselves, and would sympathise with them in their desire for such, would soon find them eager to learn her view of what was best for them; that whether this was so or not, her duty was to keep alive their own best hopes and intentions, which come at rare intervals, but fade too often for want of encouragement. I desired to be in a cond-ition to free a few poor people from the tyranny and influence of a low class of landlords and landladies; from the corrupting effect

───────────────────────────────────────

First published in the *Fortnightly Review*, November 1866 and reprinted in *Homes of the London Poor*, 1875. This chapter describes Octavia Hill's first experiences as a landlady. Numbers 1-3 Paradise Place (now Garbutt Place) in Marylebone were acquired for Octavia by John Ruskin, who paid £750 for 56-year leases. The houses are now distinguished by a blue plaque commemorating Octavia.

of continual forced communication with very degraded fellow-lodgers; from the heavy incubus of accumulated dirt: that so the never-dying hope which I find characteristic of the poor might have leave to spring, and with it such energy as might help them to help themselves. I had not great ideas of what must be done for them, my strongest endeavours were to be used to rouse habits of industry and effort, without which they must finally sink—with which they might render themselves independent of me, except as a friend and leader. The plan was one which depended on just governing more than on helping. The first point was to secure such power as would enable me to insist on some essential sanitary arrangements.

I laid the plan before Mr Ruskin, who entered into it most warmly. He at once came forward with all the money necessary, and took the whole risk of the undertaking upon himself. He showed me, however, that it would be far more useful if it could be made to pay; that a working man ought to be able to pay for his own house; that the outlay upon it ought, therefore, to yield a fair percentage on the capital invested. Thus empowered and directed, I purchased three houses in my own immediate neighbourhood. They were leasehold, subject to a small ground-rent. The unexpired term of the lease was for fifty-six years; this we purchased for £750. We spent £78 additional in making a large room at the back of my own house where I could meet the tenants from time to time. The plan has now been in operation about a year and a half; the financial result is that the scheme has paid five per cent interest on all the capital, has repaid £48 of the capital; sets of two rooms have been let for little more than the rent of one, the houses have been kept in repair, all expenses have been met for taxes, ground-rent, and insurance. In this case there is no expense for collecting rents, as I do it myself, finding it most important work; but in all the estimates I put aside the usual percentage for it, in case hereafter I may require help, and also to prove practically that it can be afforded in other cases. It should be observed that well-built houses were chosen, but they were in a dreadful state of dirt and neglect. The repairs required were mainly of a superficial and slight character: slight in regard to expense—vital as to health and comfort. The place swarmed with vermin; the papers, black with dirt, hung in long strips from the walls; the drains were stopped, the water supply was out of order. All these things were put in order, but no new appliances of any kind were added, as we had determined that our tenants should wait for these until they had proved themselves capable of taking care of them. A regular sum is set aside for repairs, and this is equally divided between the three houses; if any of it remains, after breakage and damage have been repaired, at the end of the quarter each tenant decides in turn in what way the surplus shall be spent, so as to add to the comfort of the house. This plan has worked admirably; the loss from carelessness has decreased to an amazing extent, and the lodgers prize the little comforts which they have waited for, and seem in a measure to have earned by their care, much more than those bought with more lavish expenditure. The bad debts during the whole time that the plan has been in operation have only amounted to £2 11s. 3d. Extreme punctuality and diligence in collecting rents, and a strict determination that they shall be paid regularly, have accomplished this; as a proof of which it is curious to observe that £1 3s. 3d. of the bad debts accumulated during two months that I was away in the country. I have tried to remember, when it seemed hardest, that the fulfilment of their duties was the best education for the tenants in every way. It has given them a dignity and glad feeling of honourable behaviour which has much more than compensated for the apparent harshness of the rule.

Nothing has impressed me more than the people's perception of an underlying current of sympathy through all dealings that have seemed harsh. Somehow, love and care have made themselves felt. It is also wonderful that they should prize as they do the evenness of the law that is over them. They are accustomed to alternate violence of passion and toleration of vice. They expected a greater toleration, ignorant indulgence, and frequent almsgiving, but in spite of this have recognised as a blessing a rule which is very strict, but the demands of which they know, and a government that is true in word and deed. The plan of substituting a lady for a resident landlady of the same class as her tenants is not wholly gain. The lady will probably have subtler sympathy and clearer comprehension of their needs, but she cannot give the same minute supervision that a resident landlady can. Unhappily, the advantage of such a change is, however, at present unquestionable. The influence of the majority of the lower class of people who sub-let to the poor is almost wholly injurious. That tenants should be given up to the dominion of those whose word is given and broken almost as a matter of course, whose habits and standards are very low, whose passions are violent, who have neither large hope nor clear sight, nor even sympathy, is very sad. It seems to me that a greater power is in the hands of landlords and landladies than of school-teachers—power either of life or death, physical and spiritual. It is not an unimportant question who shall wield it. There are dreadful instances in which sin is really tolerated and shared; where the lodger who will drink most with his landlord is most favoured, and many a debt overlooked, to compensate for which the price of rooms is raised; and thus the steady and sober pay more rent to make up for the losses caused by the unprincipled. But take this as an example of entirely careless rule: The owner of some cottage property in London, a small undertaker by trade, living some little distance from his property, and for the most part confining his dealings with it to a somewhat fruitless endeavour to collect the rents on a Sunday morning, in discussing the value of the property with me, said very straightforwardly, 'Yes, miss; of course there are plenty of bad debts. It's not the rents I look to, but the deaths I get out of the houses'. The man didn't mean for a moment that he knew that the state of the houses brought him a plentiful harvest of deaths, though I knew it and heard the truth ringing with awful irony through his words; but he did mean that his entire thought was of his profits—that those dependent souls and bodies were to him as nothing. Consider under such a rule what deadly quarrels spring up and deepen and widen between families compelled to live very near one another, to use many things in common, whose uneducated minds brood over and over the same slight offences, when there is no one either compulsorily to separate them, or to say some soothing word of reconciliation before the quarrel grows too serious. I have received a letter from an Irish tenant actually boasting that he 'would have taken a more manly way of settling a dispute', but that his neighbour 'showed the white feather and then retired'. I have seen that man's whole face light up and break into a smile when I suggested that a little willing kindness would be a more manly way still. And I have known him and his aunt, though boiling over with rage all the time, use steady self-control in not quarrelling for a whole month, because they knew it would spoil my holiday! Finally, they shook hands and made peace, and lived in peace many months, and, indeed, are living so now.

I could have formed no idea of the docility of the people, nor of their gratitude for small things. They are easily governed by firmness, which they respect much. I have always made a point of carefully recognising their own rights; but if a strong conviction is clearly expressed they readily adopt it, and they often accept a different idea from any they have previously desired, if it is set before them. One tenant—a silent, strong, uncringing woman, living with her seven children and her husband in one room—was certain 'there were many things she could get for the children to eat which would do them more good than another room'. I was perfectly silent. A half-pleading, half-asserting voice said: 'Don't you see I'm right, miss?' 'No,' I said; 'indeed I do not. I have been brought up to know the value of abundant good air; but of course you must do as you think best—only I am sorry.' Not a word more passed; but in a few weeks a second room was again to let, and the woman volunteered: 'She thought she'd better strive to get the rent; good air was very important, wasn't it?' Again: a man wouldn't send his children to school. Dirty, neglected, and unhappy, they destroyed many things in the house. I urged, to no purpose, that they should be sent. At last I gave him notice to leave because he refused to send them, and because he had taken three children to sleep in the room I had let for his own family only. The man was both angry and obstinate. I quietly went on with proceedings for getting rid of him. He knew I meant what I said, and he requested an interview. He owed no rent, he urged. 'No,' I replied, 'you know what a point I make of that; but it isn't quite the only thing I insist on. I cannot allow anything so wrong as this neglect of the children and overcrowding to continue where I have the power to prevent it.' He 'knew what it was just this year to fuss about the cholera, and then nobody'd care how many slep in a room; but he wasn't a coward to be frightened at the cholera, not he! And as to being bound, he wouldn't be bound—no, not to his own master that paid him wage; and it wasn't likely he would to me, when he paid rent reg'lar. The room was his; he took it, and if he paid rent he could do as he liked in it.' 'Very well,' I said; 'and the house is mine; I take it, and I must do what I think right in it; and I say that most landladies won't take in children at all, and we all know it is a good deal of loss and trouble; but I will risk these gladly if you do what you can to teach the children to be good, and careful, and industrious; and if not, you know the rule, and you must go. If you prefer liberty, and dirt, and mess, take them; but if you choose to agree to live under as good a rule as I can make it, you can stay. You have your choice.' Put in the light of a bargain the man was willing enough. Well, he'd not 'do anything contrairy, without telling me, about lodgers; and as to the children, he thought he could turn himself, and send them a bit, now his work was better'.

With the great want of rooms there is in this neighbourhood, it did not seem right to expel families, however large, inhabiting one room. Whenever from any cause a room was vacant, and a large family occupied an adjoining one, I have endeavoured to induce them to rent the two. To incoming tenants I do not let what seems decidedly insufficient accommodation. We have been able to let two rooms for four shillings and sixpence, whereas the tenants were in many cases paying four shillings for one. At first they considered it quite an unnecessary expenditure to pay more rent for a second room, however small the additional sum might be. They have gradually learnt to feel the comfort of having two rooms, and pay willingly for them.

The pecuniary success of the plan has been due to two causes. First, to the absence of middlemen; and secondly, to great strictness about punctual payment of rent. At this moment not one tenant in any of the houses owes any rent, and during the whole time, as I have said, the bad debts have been exceedingly small. The law respecting such tenancies seems very simple, and when once the method of proceeding is understood, the whole business is easily managed; and I must say most seriously that I believe it to be better to pay legal expenses for getting rid of tenants than to lose by arrears of rent—better for the whole tone of the households, kinder to the tenants. The rule should be clearly understood, and the people will respect themselves for having obeyed it. The commencement of proceedings which are known to be genuine, and not a mere threat, is usually sufficient to obtain payment of arrears: in one case only has an ejectment for rent been necessary. The great want of rooms gives the possessors of such property immense power over their lodgers. The fluctuations of work cause to respectable tenants the main difficulties in paying their rent. I have tried to help them in two ways. First, by inducing them to save: this they have done steadily, and each autumn has found them with a small fund accumulated, which has enabled them to meet the difficulties of the time when families are out of town. In the second place, I have done what I could to employ my tenants in slack seasons. I carefully set aside any work they can do for times of scarcity, and I try so to equalise in this small circle the irregularity of work, which must be more or less pernicious, and which the childishness of the poor makes doubly so. They have strangely little power of looking forward; a result is to them as nothing if it will not be perceptible till next quarter. This is very curious to me, especially as seen in connection with that large hope to which I have alluded, and which often makes me think that if I could I would carve over the houses the motto, *Spem, etiam illi habent, quibus nihil aliud restat.**

Another beautiful trait in their character is their trust; it has been quite marvellous to find how great and how ready this is. In no single case have I met with suspicion or with anything but entire confidence.

It is needless to say that there have been many minor difficulties and disappointments. Each separate person who has failed to rise and meet the help that would have been so gladly given has been a distinct loss to me; for somehow the sense of relation to them has been a very real one, and a feeling of interest and responsibility has been very strong, even where there was least that was lovely or lovable in the particular character. When they have not had sufficient energy or self control to choose the sometimes hard path that has seemed the only right one, it would have been hard to part from them, except for a hope that others would be able to lead them where I have failed.

Two distinct kinds of work depend entirely on one another if they are to bear their full fruit. There is, firstly, the simple fulfilment of a landlady's bounden duties, and uniform demand of the fulfilment of those of the tenants. We have felt ourselves bound by laws which must be obeyed, however hard obedience might often be. Then, secondly, there is the individual friendship which has grown up from intimate knowledge, and from a sense of dependence and protection. Such knowledge gives power to see the real position of families; to suggest in time the inevitable result of certain habits; to urge such measures as shall secure the education of the children and their establishment in life; to

---

*   Even those who have nothing else can have hope.

keep alive the germs of energy; to waken the gentler thought; to refuse resolutely to give any help but such as rouses self-help; to cherish the smallest lingering gleam of self-respect; and, finally, to be near with strong help should the hour of trial fall suddenly and heavily, and to give it with the hand and heart of a real old friend, who has filled many relations besides that of an alms-giver, who has long ago given far more than material help, and has thus earned the right to give this lesser help even to the most independent spirits.

The relation will finally depend on the human spirits that enter into it; like all others, it may be pernicious or helpful. It is simply a large field of labour where the labourers are few. It has the advantage over many beneficent works—that it calls out a sense of duty, and demands energetic right-doing among the poor themselves, and so purifies and stimulates them.

If any of my poorer friends chance to see this, I hope they will not think I have spoken too exclusively of what we can do for them. I have dwelt on this side of the question because it is the one we are mainly bound to consider; it is for them to think how they can help us. But I must add in gratitude that I have much to thank them for. Their energy and hope amid overwhelming difficulties have made me ashamed of my own laziness and despair. I have seen the inevitable result of faults and omissions of mine that I had never sufficiently weighed. Their patience and thankfulness are a glad cause of admiration to me continually. I trust that our relation to one another may grow better and nearer for many years.

2

Four Years' Management of a London Court

---

*F*URTHER organisation in our mode of dealing with the poor is now generally agreed to be necessary; but there is another truth less dwelt upon, yet on the due recognition of which success equally depends. I feel most deeply that the disciplining of our immense poor population must be effected by individual influence; and that this power can change it from a mob of paupers and semi-paupers into a body of self-dependent workers. It is my opinion, further, that although such influence may be brought to bear upon them in very various ways, it may be exercised in a very remarkable manner by persons undertaking the oversight and management of such houses as the poor habitually lodge in. In support of this opinion I subjoin an account of what has been actually achieved in two very poor courts in London.

About four years ago I was put in possession of three houses in one of the worst courts in Marylebone. Six other houses were bought subsequently. All were crowded with inmates. The first thing to be done was to put them in decent tenantable order. The set last purchased was a row of cottages facing a bit of desolate ground, occupied with wretched, dilapidated cow-sheds, manure

---

First published in *Macmillan's Magazine*, July 1869; reprinted in *Homes of the London Poor*, 1875. In this chapter Octavia is describing her work in Freshwater Place, Marylebone, the second group of houses acquired by John Ruskin and placed under her management. In 1866 he paid £2,880 for the freeholds of five houses in Freshwater Place and one in Old Marylebone Road which backed onto them (see p. 8). 207 Old Marylebone Road is still standing. Freshwater Place has been demolished and replaced with more modern social housing. The small garden remains.

heaps, old timber, and rubbish of every description. The houses were in a most deplorable condition—the plaster was dropping from the walls; on one staircase a pail was placed to catch the rain that fell through the roof. All the staircases were perfectly dark; the banisters were gone, having been burnt as firewood by tenants. The grates, with large holes in them, were falling forward into the rooms. The wash-house, full of lumber belonging to the landlord, was locked up; thus the inhabitants had to wash clothes, as well as to cook, eat, and sleep in their small rooms. The dustbin, standing in the front of the houses, was accessible to the whole neighbourhood, and boys often dragged from it quantities of unseemly objects and spread them over the court. The state of the drainage was in keeping with everything else. The pavement of the backyard was all broken up, and great puddles stood in it so that the damp crept up the outer walls. One large but dirty water-butt received the water laid on for the houses; it leaked, and for such as did not fill their jugs when the water came in, or who had no jugs to fill, there was no water. The former landlord's reply to one of the tenants who asked him to have an iron hoop put round the butt to prevent leakage, was, that 'if he didn't like it' (i.e. things as they were) 'he might leave'. The man to whom this was spoken—by far the best tenant in the place—is now with us, and often gives his spare time to making his room more comfortable, knowing that he will be retained, if he behaves well.

This landlord was a tradesman in a small way of business—not a cruel man, except in so far as variableness of dealing is cruelty; but he was a man without capital to spend on improvements, and lost an immense percentage of his rent by bad debts. I went over the houses with him the last day he collected his rents there, that he might introduce me to the people as the owner of the property. He took a man with him, whom, as he confided to me, he wished to pass off upon the people as a broker.* It was evident that, whether they saw through this deceit or not, they had no experience which led them to believe he intended to carry into effect the threats he uttered. The arrears of rent were enormous. I had been informed that the honest habitually pay for

---

*   The ultimate step taken to enforce payment of rent is to send in a broker to distrain (Octavia Hill's note).

the dishonest, the owner relying upon their payments to compensate for all losses; but I was amazed to find to what an extent this was the case. Six, seven, or eight weeks' rent was due from most tenants, and in some cases very much more; whereas, since I took possession of the houses (of which I collect the rents each week myself) I have never allowed a second week's rent to become due.

I think no one who has not experienced it can fully realise the almost awed sense of joy with which one enters upon such a possession as that above described, conscious of having the power to set it, even partially, in order. Hopes, indeed, there are which one dares scarcely hope; but at once one has power to say, 'Break out a window there in that dark corner; let God's light and air in'; or, 'Trap that foul drain, and shut the poisonous miasma out'; and one has moral power to say, by deeds which speak louder than words, 'Where God gives me authority, this, which you in your own hearts know to be wrong, shall not go on. I would not set my conviction, however strong it might be, against your judgment of right; but when you are doing what I know your own conscience condemns, I, now that I have the power, will enforce right; but first I will try whether I cannot lead you, yourselves, to arise and cast out sin—helping your wavering and sorely tried will by mine, which is untempted'.

As soon as I entered into possession, each family had an opportunity of doing better: those who would not pay, or who led clearly immoral lives, were ejected. The rooms they vacated were cleansed; the tenants who showed signs of improvement moved into them, and thus, in turn, an opportunity was obtained for having each room distempered and painted. The drains were put in order, a large slate cistern was fixed, the wash-house was cleared of its lumber, and thrown open on stated days to each tenant in turn. The roof, the plaster, the woodwork were repaired; the staircase-walls were distempered; new grates were fixed; the layers of paper and rag (black with age) were torn from the windows, and glass was put in; out of 192 panes, only eight were found unbroken. The yard and footpath were paved.

The rooms, as a rule, were re-let at the same prices at which they had been let before; but tenants with large families were counselled to take two rooms, and for these much less was charged than if let singly: this plan I continue to pursue.

Incoming tenants are not allowed to take a decidedly insufficient quantity of room, and no sub-letting is permitted. The elder girls are employed three times a week in scrubbing the passages in the houses, for the cleaning of which the landlady is responsible. For this work they are paid, and by it they learn habits of cleanliness. It is, of course, within the authority of the landlady also to insist on cleanliness of wash-houses, yards, staircases, and staircase-windows; and even to remonstrate concerning the rooms themselves if they are habitually dirty.

The pecuniary result has been very satisfactory. Five per cent interest has been paid on all the capital invested. A fund for the repayment of capital is accumulating. A liberal allowance has been made for repairs; and here I may speak of the means adopted for making the tenants careful about breakage and waste. The sum allowed yearly for repairs is fixed for each house, and if it has not all been spent in restoring and replacing, the surplus is used for providing such additional appliances as the tenants themselves desire. It is therefore to their interest to keep the expenditure for repairs as low as possible; and instead of committing the wanton damage common among tenants of their class, they are careful to avoid injury, and very helpful in finding economical methods of restoring what is broken or worn out, often doing little repairs of their own accord.

From the proceeds of the rent, also, interest has been paid on the capital spent in building a large room where the tenants can assemble. Classes are held there—for boys, twice weekly; for girls, once; a singing class has just been established. A large work-class for married women and elder girls meets once a week. A glad sight it is—the large room filled with the eager, merry faces of the girls, from which those of the older, careworn women catch a reflected light. It is a good time for quiet talk with them as we work, and many a neighbourly feeling is called out among the women as they sit together on the same bench, lend one another cotton or needles, are served by the same hand, and look to the same person for direction. The babies are a great bond of union: I have known the very women who not long before had been literally fighting, sit at the work-class busily and earnestly comparing notes of their babies' respective history. That a consciousness of corporate life is developed in them is shown by the not infrequent use of the expression 'One of us'.

Among the arrangements conducive to comfort and health, I may mention that instead of the clothes being hung, as formerly, out of front windows down against the wall, where they could not be properly purified, the piece of ground in front of the houses is used as a drying-ground during school hours. The same place is appropriated as a playground, not only for my younger tenants, but for the children of the neighbouring courts. It is a space walled round, where they can play in safety. Hitherto, games at trap, bat and ball, swinging, skipping, and singing a few Kinder-Garten songs with movements in unison, have been the main diversions. But I have just established drill for the boys, and a drum and fife band. Unhappily, the mere business connected with the working of the houses has occupied so much time, that the playground has been somewhat neglected; yet it is a most important part of the work. The evils of the streets and courts are too evident to need explanation. In the playground are gathered together children habitually dirty, quarrelsome, and violent. They come wholly ignorant of games, and have hardly self-control enough to play at any which have an object or require effort. Mere senseless, endless repetition is at best their diversion. Often the games are only repetitions of questionable sentences. For instance, what is to be said of a game the whole of which consists in singing, 'Here comes my father all down the hill, all down the hill' (over and over again), and replying, 'We won't get up for his ugly face—ugly face' (repeated *ad libitum*)? Then come the mother, the sister, the brother, to whom the same words are addressed. Finally the lover comes, to whom the greeting is, 'We will get up for his pretty face'. This was, perhaps, the best game the children knew, yet, in as far as it had any meaning or influence, it must be bad. Compare it, or the wild, lawless fighting or gambling, with a game at trap, arranged with ordered companions, definite object, and progressive skill. The moral influence depends, however, on having ladies who will go to the playground, teach games, act as umpires, know and care for the children. These I hope to find more and more. Until now, except at rare intervals, the playground has been mainly useful for the fresh air it affords to the children who are huddled together by night in small rooms, in the surrounding courts. The more respectable parents keep them indoors, even in the day time, after school-hours, to prevent their meeting with bad companions.

Mr Ruskin, to whom the whole undertaking owes its existence, has had trees planted in the playground, and creepers against the houses. In May, we have a May-pole or a throne covered with flowers for the May-queen and her attendants. The sweet luxuriance of the spring flowers is more enjoyed in that court than would readily be believed. Some months after the first festival the children were seen sticking a few faded flowers into a crevice in the wall, saying they wanted to make it 'like it was the day we had the May-pole'.

I have tried, as far as opportunity has permitted, to develop the love of beauty among my tenants. The poor of London need joy and beauty in their lives. There is no more true and eternal law to be recognised about them than that which Mr Dickens shows in *Hard Times*—the fact that every man has an imagination which needs development and satisfaction. Mr Slearey's speech, 'People mutht be amoothed, Thquire,' is often recalled to my mind in dealing with the poor. They work hard; their lives are monotonous; they seek low places of amusement; they break out into lawless 'sprees'. Almost all amusements—singing, dancing, acting, expeditions into the country, eating and drinking—are liable to abuse; no rules are subtle enough to prevent their leading to harm. But if a lady can know the individuals, and ask them as her invited guests to any of these, an innate sense of honour and respect preserves the tone through the whole company. Indeed, there can hardly be a more proudly thankful moment than that, when we see these many people, to whom life is dull and full of anxiety, gathered together around us for holy, happy Christmas festivities, or going out to some fair and quiet spot in the bright summer time, bound to one another by the sense of common relationship, preserved unconsciously from wrong by the presence of those whom they love and who love them. Such intervals of bright joy are easily arranged by friends for friends; but if strangers are invited *en masse* it is difficult to keep any of these recreations innocent.

All these ways of meeting are invaluable as binding us together; still they would avail little were it not for the work by which we are connected, for the individual care each member of the little circle receives. Week by week, when the rents are collected, an opportunity of seeing each family separately occurs. There are a multitude of matters to attend to. First, there is the mere outside business—rent to be received, requests from the tenant respecting repairs to be considered; sometimes decisions touching the behaviour of other tenants to be made, sometimes rebukes for untidiness to be administered. Then come the sad or joyful remarks about health or work, the little histories of the week. Sometimes grave questions arise about important changes in the life of the family—shall a daughter go to service? or shall the sick child be sent to a hospital? etc.

Sometimes violent quarrels must be allayed. Much may be done in this way, so ready is the response in these affectionate natures to those whom they trust and love. For instance: two women among my tenants fought; one received a dreadful kick, the other had hair torn from her head. They were parted by a lad who lived in the house. The women occupied adjoining rooms, they met in the passages, they used the same yard and wash-house, endless were the opportunities of collision while they were engaged with each other. For ten days I saw them repeatedly; I could in no way reconcile them—words of rage and recrimination were all that they uttered; while the hair, which had been carefully preserved by the victim, was continually exhibited to me as a sufficient justification for lasting anger. One was a cold, hard, self-satisfied, well-to-do woman; the other a nervous, affectionate, passionate, very poor Irishwoman. Now it happened that in speaking to the latter one evening, I mentioned my own grief at the quarrel; a look of extreme pain came over her face—it was a new idea to her that I should care. That, and no sense of the wrong of indulging an evil passion, touched her. The warm-hearted creature at once promised to shake hands with her adversary; but she had already taken out a summons against the other for assault, and did not consider she could afford to make up the quarrel because it implied losing the two shillings the summons had cost. I told her the loss was a mere nothing to her if weighed in the balance with peace, but that I would willingly pay it. It only needed that one of the combatants should make the first step towards reconciliation for the other (who, indeed, rather dreaded answering the summons) to meet her half-way. They are good neighbours now of some months' standing. A little speech, which shows the character of the Irishwoman, is worth recording. Acknowledging to me that she was very passionate, she said: 'My husband never takes my part when I'm in my tanthrums, and I'm that mad with him; but, bless you, I love him all the better afterwards; he knows well enough it would only make me worse'. I may here observe that the above-mentioned two shillings is the only money I ever had to give to either woman. It is on such infinitesimally small actions that the success of the whole work rests.

My tenants are mostly of a class far below that of mechanics. They are, indeed, of the very poor. And yet, although the gifts they have received have been next to nothing, none of the families who have passed under my care during the whole four-years have continued in what is called 'distress', except such as have been unwilling to exert themselves. Those who will not exert the necessary self-control cannot avail themselves of the means of livelihood held out to them. But, for those who are willing, some small assistance in the form of work has, from time to time, been provided—not much, but sufficient to keep them from want or despair. The following will serve as an instance of the sort of help given and its proportion to the results.

Alice, a single woman, of perhaps fifty-five years, lodged with a man and his wife—the three in one room—just before I obtained full possession of the houses. Alice, not being able to pay her rent, was turned into the street, where Mrs S. (my playground superintendent) met her, crying dreadfully.

It was Saturday, and I had left town till Monday. Alice had neither furniture to pawn nor friends to help her; the workhouse alone lay before her. Mrs S. knew that I esteemed her as a sober, respectable, industrious woman, and therefore she ventured to express to Alice's landlord the belief that I would not let him lose money if he would let her go back to her lodging till Monday, when I should return home, thus risking for me a possible loss of fourpence—not very ruinous to me, and a sum not impossible for Alice to repay in the future.

I gave Alice two days' needlework, then found her employment in tending a bedridden cottager in the country, whose daughter (in service) paid for the nursing. Five weeks she was there, working and saving her money. On her return I lent her what more she required to buy furniture, and then she took a little room direct from me. Too blind to do much household work, but able to sew almost mechanically, she just earns her daily bread by making sailors' shirts, but her little home is her own, and she loves it dearly; and, having tided over that time of trial, Alice can live—has paid all her debts too, and is more grateful than she would have been for many gifts.

At one time I had a room to let which was ninepence a week cheaper than the one she occupied. I proposed to her to take it; it had, however, a different aspect, getting less of the southern and western sunlight. Alice hesitated long, and asked *me* to decide, which I declined to do; for, as I told her, her moving would suit my arrangements rather better. She, hearing that, wished to move; but I begged her to make her decision wholly irrespective of my plans. At last she said, very wistfully, 'Well, you see, miss, it's between ninepence and the sun'. Sadly enough, ninepence had to outweigh the sun.

My tenants are, of course, encouraged to save their money. It should, however, be remarked that I have never succeeded in getting them to save for old age. The utmost I have achieved is that they lay by sufficient either to pay rent in times of scarcity, to provide clothes for girls going to service, or boots, or furniture, or even to avail themselves of opportunities of advancement which must be closed to them if they had not a little reserve fund to meet expenses of the change.

One great advantage arising from the management of the houses is that they form a test-place, in which people may prove themselves worthy of higher situations. Not a few of the tenants have been persons who had sunk below the stratum where once they were known, and some of these, simply by proving their character, have been enabled to regain their former stations. One man, twenty years ago, had been a gentleman's servant, had saved money, gone into business, married, failed, and then found himself out of the groove of work. When I made his acquaintance he was earning a miserable pittance for his wife and seven unhealthy children, and all the nine souls were suffering and sinking unknown. After watching, and proving him for three years, I was able to recommend him to a gentleman in the country, where now the whole family are profiting, by having six rooms instead of one, fresh air, and regular wages.

But it is far easier to be helpful than to have patience and self-control sufficient, when the times come, for seeing suffering and not relieving it. And yet the main tone of action must be severe. There is much of rebuke and repression needed, although a deep and silent under-current of sympathy and pity may flow beneath.

If the rent is not ready, notice to quit must be served. The money is then almost always paid, when the notice is, of course, withdrawn. Besides this inexorable demand for rent (never to be relaxed without entailing cumulative evil on the defaulter, and setting a bad example, too readily followed by others), there must be a perpetual crusade carried on against small evils—very wearing sometimes. It is necessary to believe that in thus setting in order certain spots on God's earth, still more in presenting to a few of His children a somewhat higher standard of right, we are doing His work, and that He will not permit us to lose sight of His large laws, but will rather make them evident to us through the small details.

The resolution to watch pain which cannot be radically relieved except by the sufferer himself is most difficult to maintain. Yet it is wholly necessary in certain cases not to help. Where a man persistently refuses to exert himself, eternal help is worse than useless. By withholding gifts we say to him in action more mournful than words: 'You will not do better. I was ready—I will be ready whenever you come to yourself; but until then you must pursue your own course'. This attitude has often to be taken; but it usually proves a summons to a more energetic spirit, producing nobler effort in great matters, just as the notice to quit arouses resolution and self-denial in pecuniary concerns.

Coming together so much as we do for business with mutual duties, for recreation with common joy, each separate want or fault having been dealt with as it arose, it will be readily understood that in such a crisis as that which periodically occurs in the East-end of London, instead of being unprepared, I feel myself somewhat like an officer at the head of a well-controlled little regiment, or, more accurately, like a country proprietor with a moderate number of well-ordered tenants.

For, firstly, my people are numbered; not merely counted, but known, man, woman, and child. I have seen their self-denying efforts to pay rent in time of trouble, or their reckless extravagance in seasons of abundance; their patient labour, or their failure to use the self-control necessary to the performance of the more remunerative kinds of work; their efforts to keep their children at school, or their selfish, lazy way of living on their children's earnings. Could anyone, going suddenly among even so small a number as these thirty-four families—however much penetration and zeal he might possess—know so accurately as I what kind of assistance could be really helpful, and not corrupting? And if positive gifts must be resorted to, who can give them with so little pain to the proud spirit, so little risk of undermining the feeble one, as the friend of old standing?—the friend, moreover, who has rigorously exacted the fulfilment of their duty in punctual payment of rent; towards whom, therefore, they might feel that they had done what they could while strength lasted, and need not surely be ashamed to receive a little bread in time of terrible want?

But it ought hardly ever to come to an actual doling out of bread or alms of any kind. During the winter of 1867-68, while the newspapers were ringing with appeals in consequence of the distress prevalent in the metropolis, being on the Continent, and unable to organise more satisfactory schemes of assistance, I wrote to the ladies who were superintending the houses for me, to suggest that a small fund (which had accumulated from the rents, after defraying expenses and paying interest) should be distributed in gifts to any of the families who might be in great poverty. The answer was that there were none requiring such help. Now, how did this come to pass?

Simply through the operation of the various influences above described. The tenants never having been allowed to involve themselves in debt to rent (now and then being supplied with employment to enable them to pay it), they were free from one of the greatest drags upon a poor family, and had, moreover, in times of prosperity been able really to save. It is but too often the case that, even when prosperous times come, working people cannot lay by, because then they have to pay off arrears of rent. The elder girls, too, were either in service or quite ready to go; and so steady, tidy, and respectable as to be able to fill good situations. This was owing, in many cases, to a word or two spoken long before, urging their longer attendance at school, or to their having had a few happy and innocent amusements provided for them, which had satisfied their natural craving for recreation, and had prevented their breaking loose in search of it. Health had been secured by an abundance of air, light, and water. Even among this very lowest class of people, I had found individuals whom I could draft from my lodging-houses into resident situations (transplanting them thus at once into a higher trade), simply because I was able to say, 'I know them to be honest, I know them to be clean'. Think of what this mere fact of *being known* is to the poor!

You may say, perhaps, 'This is very well as far as you and your small knot of tenants are concerned, but how does it help us to deal with the vast masses of poor in our great towns?' I reply, 'Are not the great masses made up of many small knots? Are not the great towns divisible into small districts? Are there not people who would gladly come forward to undertake the systematic supervision of some house or houses, if they could get authority from the owner? And why should there not be some way of registering such supervision, so that, bit by bit, as more volunteers should come forward, the whole metropolis might be mapped out, all the blocks fitting in like little bits of mosaic to form one connected whole?'

The success of the plan does not depend entirely upon the houses being the property of the superintendent. I would urge people, if possible, to purchase the houses of which they undertake the charge; but, if they cannot, they may yet do a valuable little bit of work by registering a distinct declaration that they will supervise such and such a house, or row, or street; that if they have to relinquish the work they will say so; that if it becomes too much for them, they will ask for help; that anyone desiring information about the families dwelling in the houses they manage may apply to them.

It is well known that the societies at work among the poor are so numerous, and labour so independently of each other, that, at present, many sets of people may administer relief to a given family in one day, and perhaps not one go near them again for a long interval; yet each society may be quite systematic in its own field of operation. It seems to me, that though each society might like to go its own way (and, perhaps, to supply wants which the house-overseer might think it best to leave unsupplied), they might at least feel it an advantage to know of a recognised authority, from whom particulars could be learned respecting relief already given, and the history of the families in question.

Any persons accustomed to visit among the poor in a large district would, I believe, when confining themselves to a much smaller one, be led, if not to very unexpected conclusions, at least to very curious problems. In dealing with a large number of cases the urgency is so great one passes over the most difficult questions to work where sight is clear; and one is apt to forget

Sissy Jupe's quick sympathetic perception that percentage signifies literally nothing to the friends of the special sufferer, who surely is not worth less than a sparrow. The individual case, if we cared enough for it, would often give us the key to many.

Whoever will limit his gaze to a few persons, and try to solve the problem of their lives—planning, for instance, definitely, how he, even with superior advantages of education, self-control, and knowledge, could bring up a given family on given wages, allowing the smallest amount conceivably sufficient for food, rent, clothes, fuel, and the rest—he may find it in most cases a much more difficult thing than he had ever thought, and sometimes, maybe, an impossibility. It may lead to strange self-questioning about wages. Again, if people will watch carefully the different effect of self-help and of alms, how the latter, like the outdoor relief system under the old Poor-Law, tends to lower wages, and undermines the providence of the poor, it may make them put some searching questions to themselves upon the wisdom of backing up wages with gifts. Then they may begin to consider practically whether in their own small sphere they can form no schemes of help, which shall be life-giving, stimulating hope, energy, foresight, self-denial, and choice of right rather than wrong expenditure.

They may earnestly strive to discover plans of help which shall free them from the oppressive responsibility of deciding whether aid is deserved—a question often complicated inextricably with another, namely, whether at a given moment there is a probability of reformation. All of us have felt the impossibility of deciding either question fairly, yet we have been convinced that gifts coming at the wrong time are often deadly. Earnest workers feel a heavy weight on their hearts and consciences from the conviction that the old command, 'Judge not,' is a divine one, and yet that the distribution of alms irrespective of character is fatal. These difficulties lead to variable action, which is particularly disastrous with the poor. But there are plans which cultivate the qualities wherein they are habitually wanting, namely, self-control, energy, prudence, and industry; and such plans, if we will do our part, may be ready at any moment for even the least deserving, and for those who have fallen lowest.

Further details as to modes of help must vary infinitely with circumstances and character. But I may mention a few laws which become clearer and clearer to me as I work.

It is best strictly to enforce fulfilment of all such duties as payment of rent, etc.

It is far better to give work than either money or goods.

It is most helpful of all to strengthen by sympathy and counsel the energetic effort which shall bear fruit in time to come.

It is essential to remember that each man has his own view of his life, and must be free to fulfil it; that in many ways he is a far better judge of it than we, as he has lived through and felt what we have only seen. Our work is rather to bring him to the point of considering, and to the spirit of judging rightly, than to consider or judge for him.

The poor of London (as of all large towns) need the development of every power which can open to them noble sources of joy.

3

Landlords and Tenants in London

HREE ladies were standing, not long ago, in a poor and dingy court in London, when a group of dirty-faced urchins exclaimed, in a tone, partly of impudence and partly of fun: 'What a lot o' landladies this morning!'

The words set me thinking, for I felt that the boys' mirth was excited, not only by the number of landladies (or of ladies acting as such), but also, probably, by the contrast between these ladies and the landladies they usually saw. For the landlady to the London poor is too often a struggling, cheated, much worried, long-suffering woman; soured by constant dealing with untrustworthy people; embittered by loss; a prey to the worst lodgers, whom she allows to fall into debt, and is afraid to turn out, lest she should lose the amount they owe her; without spirit or education to enable her to devise improvements, or capital to execute them—never able, in short, to use the power given her by her position to bring order into the lives of her tenants; being, indeed, too frequently entirely under their control. There is a numerous class of landladies worse even than this—bullying, violent, passionate, revengeful, and cowardly. They alternately cajole and threaten, but rarely intend to carry out either their promises or their threats. Severe without principle, weakly

First published in *Macmillan's Magazine*, October 1871; reprinted in *Homes of the London Poor*, 1875. Octavia is describing her work in Barrett's Court (now St Christopher's Place) which runs from Oxford Street to Wigmore Street, opposite to Bond Street underground station. Elsewhere in her writings she refers to it under the pseudonym of 'Blank Court'. To Octavia's annoyance, seven of the houses were declared insanitary in 1873 by the Medical Officer of Health, in spite of all her good work, and had to be pulled down and re-built.

indulgent towards evil, given to lying and swearing, too covetous to be drunken, yet indulgent to any lodger who will 'treat' them; their influence is incalculably mischievous.

Ought this to be the idea suggested by the word 'landlady' to the poor of our cities? The old word 'landlord' is a proud one to many an English gentleman, who holds dominion over the neat cottage, with its well-stocked garden; over the comfortable farm-house; over broad, sloping parks, and rich farm-lands. It is a delight to him to keep thus fair the part of the earth over which it has been given him to rule. And, as to his people, he would think it shameful to receive the rents from his well-managed estates in the country, year by year, without some slight recognition of his tenantry—at least on birthdays or at Christmas.

But where are the owners, or lords, or ladies, of most courts like that in which I stood with my two fellow-workers? Who holds dominion there? Who heads the tenants there? If any among the nobly born, or better educated, own them, do they bear the mark of their hands? And if they do *not* own them, might they not do so? There are in those courts as loyal English hearts as ever loved or reverenced the squire in the village, only they have been so forgotten. Dark under the level ground, in kitchens damp with foulest moisture, there they huddle in multitudes, and no one loves or raises them. It must not be thought that the overworked clergymen and missionaries, heroic as they often are, can do all that might be done for them. They count their flock by thousands, and these people want watching one by one. The clergy have no control over these places, nor have they half the power of directing labour to useful ends, which those might have who owned the houses, and were constantly brought into direct contact with the people.

How this relation of landlord and tenant might be established in some of the lowest districts of London, and with what results, I am about to describe by relating what has been done in the last two years in a court in Marylebone. I have already given an account of my former efforts to establish this relation on a healthy footing in another London court; of the details of my plan of action; and of its success. I am not, therefore, in what follows, putting forth anything new in its main idea, but am simply insisting on principles of the truth of which every day's experience only makes me the more deeply assured, and recounting the history of an attempt to spread those principles to a class still lower than that alluded to in my former paper.

It was near the end of 1869 that I first heard that a good many houses in a court near my own house were to be disposed of. Eventually, in the course of that year, six ten-roomed houses were bought by the Countess of Ducie, and five more by another lady, and placed partially under my care. I was especially glad to obtain some influence here, as I knew this place to be one of the worst in Marylebone; its inhabitants were mainly costermongers and small hawkers, and were almost the poorest class of those amongst our population who have any settled home, the next grade below them being vagrants who sleep in common lodging-houses; and I knew that its moral standing was equally low. Its reputation had long been familiar to me; for when unruly and hopeless tenants were sent away from other houses in the district, I had often heard that they had gone to this court, the tone in which it was said implying that they had now sunk to the lowest depths of degradation. A lawyer friend had also said to me, on hearing that it was proposed to buy houses there, 'That court! why, that is the place one is always noticing in the police reports for its rows'.

Yet its outward appearance would not have led a casual observer to guess its real character. It is not far from Cavendish Square, and daily in the season, scores of carriages, with their gaily-dressed occupants, pass the end of it. Should such look down it, they would little divine its inner life. Seen from the outside, and in the daytime, it is a quiet-looking place, the houses a moderate size, and the space between them tolerably wide. It has no roadway, but is nicely enough paved, and old furniture stands out for sale on the pavement, in front of the few shops.

But if anyone had entered those houses with me two years ago, he would have seen enough to surprise and horrify him. In many of the houses the dustbins were utterly unapproachable, and cabbage-leaves, stale fish, and every sort of dirt were lying in the passages and on the stairs; in some the back kitchen had been used as a dustbin, but had not been emptied for years, and the dust filtered through into the front kitchens, which were the sole living and sleeping rooms of some families; in some the kitchen stairs were many inches thick with dirt, which was so hardened that a shovel had to be used to get it off; in some there was hardly any water to be had; the wood was eaten and broken away; windows were smashed; and the rain was coming through the roofs. At night it was still worse; and during the first winter I had to collect the rents chiefly then, as the inhabitants, being principally costermongers, were out nearly all day, and they were afraid to entrust their rent to their neighbours. It was then that I saw the houses in their most dreadful aspect. I well remember wet, foggy Monday nights, when I turned down the dingy court, past the brilliantly lighted public-house at the corner, past the old furniture outside the shops, and dived into the dark yawning passage ways. The front doors stood open day and night, and as I felt my way down the kitchen-stairs, broken and rounded by the hardened mud upon them, the foul smells which the heavy foggy air would not allow to rise met me as I descended, and the plaster rattled down with a hollow sound as I groped along. It was truly appalling to think that there were human beings who lived habitually in such an atmosphere, with such surroundings. Sometimes I had to open the kitchen door myself, after knocking several times in vain, when a woman, quite drunk, would be lying on the floor on some black mass which served as a bed; sometimes, in answer to my knocks, a half drunken man would swear, and thrust the rent-money out to me through a chink of the door, placing his foot against it, so as to prevent it from opening wide enough to admit me. Always it would be shut again without a light being offered to guide me up the pitch-dark stairs. Such was the court in the winter of 1869. Truly a wild, lawless, desolate little kingdom to come to rule over.

On what principles was I to rule these people? On the same that I had already tried, and tried with success, in other places, and which I may sum up as the two following: firstly, to demand a strict fulfilment of their duties to me—one of the chief of which would be the punctual payment of rent; and secondly, to endeavour to be so unfailingly just and patient, that they should learn to trust the rule that was over them.

With regard to details, I would make a few improvements at once—such, for example, as the laying on of water and repairing of dustbins; but, for the most part, improvements should be made only by degrees, as the people became more capable of valuing and not abusing them. I would have the rooms distempered and thoroughly cleansed as they became vacant, and then they should be offered to the more cleanly of the tenants. I would have such repairs as were not immediately needed used as a means of giving work to the men in times of distress. I would draft the occupants of the underground kitchens into the upstair rooms, and would ultimately convert the kitchens into bath-rooms and wash-houses. I would have the landlady's portion of the house—*i.e.* the stairs and passages—at once repaired and distempered; and they should be regularly scrubbed, and, as far as possible, made models of cleanliness; for I knew from former experience that the example of this would, in time, silently spread itself to the rooms themselves, and that payment for this work would give me some hold over the elder girls. I would collect savings personally, not trust to their being taken to distant banks or saving clubs. And, finally, I knew that I should learn to feel these people as my friends, and so should instinctively feel the same respect for their privacy and their independence, and should treat them with the same courtesy that I should show towards any other personal friends. There would be no interfer-ence, no entering their rooms uninvited, no offer of money or the necessaries of life. But when occasion presented itself, I should give them any help I could, such as I might offer without insult to other friends—sympathy in their distresses; advice, help, and counsel in their difficulties; introductions that might be of use to them; means of education; visits to the country; a loan of books; a bunch of flowers brought on purpose; an invitation to any entertainment, in a room built at the back of my own house, which would be likely to give them pleasure. I am convinced that one of the evils of much that is done for the poor springs from the want of delicacy felt, and courtesy shown, towards them, and that we cannot beneficially help them in any spirit different to that in which we help those who are better off. The help may differ in amount, because their needs are greater. It should not differ in kind.

To sum up: my endeavours in ruling these people should be to maintain perfect strictness in our business relations, perfect respectfulness in our personal relations.

These principles of government and plans of action were not theoretical; they had not been *thought out* in the study, but had been *worked out* in the course of practical dealings with individ-ual cases. And though I am able thus to formulate them, I want it understood that they are essentially living, that they are not mere dead rules, but principles, the application of which is varying from day to day. I can say, for example, 'It is our plan to keep some repairs as employment for men out of work'; but it needs the true instinct to apply this plan beneficially: the time to give the work, its kind, its amount, above all the mode of offering it, have to be felt out fresh on each fresh occasion, and the circumstances and characters vary so that each case is new.

The practical carrying out in any court of these various plans of action involved, as may readily be imagined, a great deal of personal supervision. Hence the 'lot o' landladies' which excited the attention of the street boys. Several ladies, whether owners of houses or not, have worked there energetically with me since the property was bought; and when I use the word 'we', I would have it understood to apply to these ladies and myself; it is often upon them that much of the detail of the work devolves.

But to proceed with the history of this court. Our first step on obtaining possession was to call on all the inhabitants to establish our claim to receive rents. We accepted or refused the people as tenants, made their acquaintance, and learnt all they might be disposed to tell us about themselves and their families. We came upon strange scenes sometimes. In one room a handsome, black, tangle-haired, ragged boy and girl, of about nine and ten, with wild dark eyes, were always to be found, sometimes squatting near the fire, watching a great black pot, sometimes amusing themselves with cutting paper into strips with scissors. It was difficult to extract a word; the money and dirty rent-book were generally pushed to us in silence. No grown person was ever to be seen. For months I never saw these children in the open air. Often they would lie in bed all day long; and I believe they were too ignorant and indolent to care to leave the house except at night, when the boy, as we afterwards found, would creep like a cat along the roofs of the outbuildings to steal lumps of coal from a neighbouring shed.

At one room we had to call again and again, always finding the door locked. At last, after weeks of vain effort, I found the woman who owned the room at home. She was sitting on the floor at tea with another woman, the tea being served on an inverted hamper. I sat down on an opposite hamper, which was the only other piece of furniture in the room, and told her I was sorry that I had never been able to make her acquaintance before. To which she replied, with rather a grand air and a merry twinkle in her eye, that she had been 'unavoidably absent'; in other words, some weeks in prison—not a rare occurrence for her.

When we set about our repairs and alterations, there was much that was discouraging. The better class of people in the court were hopeless of any permanent improvement. When one of the tenants of the shops saw that we were sending workmen into the empty rooms, he said considerately, 'I'll tell you what it is, Miss, it'll cost you a lot o' money to repair them places, and it's no good. The women's 'eads 'll be druv through the door panels again in no time, and the place is good enough for such cattle as them there'. But we were not to be deterred.

On the other hand, we were not to be hurried in our action by threats. These were not wanting. For no sooner did the tenants see the workmen about than they seemed to think that if they only clamoured enough, they would get their own rooms put to rights. Nothing had been done for years. Now, they thought, was their opportunity. More than one woman locked me in her room with her, the better to rave and storm. She would shake the rent in her pocket to tempt me with the sound of the money, and roar out 'that never a farthing of it would she pay till her grate was set', or her floor was mended, as the case might be. Perfect silence would make her voice drop lower and lower, until at last she would stop, wondering that no violent answers were hurled back at her, and a pause would ensue. I felt that promises would be little believed in, and, besides, I wished to feel free to do as much, and only as much, as seemed best to me; so that my plan was to trust to my deeds to speak for themselves, and inspire confidence as time went on. In such a pause, therefore, I once said to a handsome, gipsy-like Irishwoman, 'How long have you lived here?' 'More than four years', she replied, her voice swelling again at the remembrance of her wrongs; 'and always was a good tenant, and paid my way, and never a thing done! And my grate,' etc., etc., etc. 'And how long have I had the houses?' 'Well, I suppose since Monday week', in a gruff but somewhat mollified tone. 'Very well, Mrs. L—, just think over quietly what has been done in the houses since then; and if you like to leave, and think you can suit yourself better, I am glad you should make yourself comfortable. Meantime, of course, while you stay you pay rent. I will call for it this evening if it doesn't suit you to pay now. Good morning.'

Almost immediately after the purchase of the houses, we had the accumulated refuse of years carted away, the pavements in the yards and front areas were repaired, dustbins cleared, the drains put in order, and water supplied. Such improvements as these are tolerably unspoilable, but for any of a more destructible nature it was better to wait. The importance of advancing slowly, and of gaining some hold over the people as a necessary accompaniment to any real improvement in their dwellings, was perpetually apparent. Their habits were so degraded that we had to work a change in these before they would make any proper use of the improved surroundings we were prepared to give them. We had locks torn off, windows broken, drains stopped, dustbins misused in every possible manner; even pipes broken, and water-taps wrenched away. This was sometimes the result of carelessness, and deeply-rooted habit of dirt and untidiness; sometimes the damage was wilful. Our remedy was to watch the right moment for furnishing these appliances, to persevere in supplying them, and to get the people by degrees to work with us for their preservation. I have learned to know that people are ashamed to abuse a place they find cared for. They will add dirt to dirt till a place is pestilential, but the more they find done for it, the more they will respect it, till at last order and cleanliness prevail. It is this feeling of theirs, coupled with the fact that they do not like those whom they have learned to love, and whose standard is higher than their own, to see things which would grieve them, which has enabled us to accomplish nearly every reform of outward things that we have achieved; so that the surest way to have any place kept clean is to go through it often yourself. First I go at regular times, and then they clean to receive me, and have the pleasure of preparing for me, and seeing my satisfaction; then I go at unexpected times, to raise them to the power of having it always clean.

Our plan of removing the inhabitants of the miserable underground kitchens to rooms in the upper parts of the houses did not, strange as it may seem, meet with any approbation at first. They had been so long in the semi-darkness, that they felt it an effort to move. One woman, in particular, I remember pleaded with me hard to let her stop, saying, 'My bits of things won't look *anything* if you bring them to the light'. By degrees, however, we effected the change.

I mentioned in my summary of our plan of operations, our custom of using some of the necessary, yet not immediately wanted repairs, as a means of affording work to the tenants in slack times. I lay great stress upon this. Though the men are not mechanics, there are many rough jobs of plastering, distemper-ing, glazing, or sweeping away and removing rubbish which they can do. When, therefore, a tenant is out of work, instead of reducing his energy by any gifts of money, we simply, whenever the funds at our disposal allow it, employ him in restoring and purifying the houses. And what a difference five shillings' worth of work in a bad week will make to a family! The father, instead of idling listlessly at the corner of the street, sets busily and happily to work, prepares the whitewash, mends the plaster, distempers the room; the wife bethinks herself of having a turn-out of musty corners or drawers—untouched, maybe, for months—of cleaning her windows, perhaps even of putting up a clean blind; and thus a sense of decency, the hope of beginning afresh and doing better, comes like new life into the home.

The same cheering and encouraging sort of influence, though in a less degree, is exercised by our plan of having a little band of scrubbers.

We have each passage scrubbed twice a week by one of the elder girls. The sixpence thus earned is a stimulus, and they often take an extreme interest in the work itself. One little girl was so proud of her first cleaning that she stood two hours watching her passage lest the boys, whom she considered as the natural enemies of order and cleanliness, should spoil it before I came to see it. And one woman remarked to her neighbour how nice the stairs looked. 'They haven't been cleaned', she added, 'since ever I came into this house'. She had been there six years! The effect of these clean passages frequently spreads to the rooms, as the dark line of demarcation between the cleaned passage and the still dirty room arouses the attention, and begins to trouble the minds of its inmates.

Gradually, then, these various modes of dealing with our little realm began to tell. Gradually the people began to trust us; and gradually the houses were improved. The sense of quiet power and sympathy soon made itself felt, and less and less was there any sign of rudeness or violence towards ourselves. Even before the first winter was over many a one would hurry to light us up the stairs, and instead of my having the rent-book and money thrust to me through the half-open door, and being kept from possible entrance by a firmly-planted foot, my reception would be, 'Oh, can't you come in, Miss, and sit down for a bit?' Little by little the houses were renovated, the grates reset, the holes in the floors repaired, the cracking, dirty plaster replaced by a clean smooth surface, the heaps of rubbish removed, and we progressed towards order.

Amongst the many benefits which the possession of the houses enables us to confer on the people, perhaps one of the most important is our power of saving them from neighbours who would render their lives miserable. It is a most merciful thing to protect the poor from the pain of living in the next room to drunken, disorderly people. 'I am dying', said an old woman to me the other day: 'I wish you would put me where I can't hear S—beating his wife. Her screams are awful. And B—, too, he do come in so drunk. Let me go over the way to No. 30.' Our success depends on duly arranging the inmates: not too many children in any one house, so as to overcrowd it; not too few, so as to overcrowd another; not two bad people side by side, or they drink together; not a terribly bad person beside a very respectable one.

Occasionally we come upon people whose lives are so good and sincere, that it is only by such services, and the sense of our friendship, we can help them at all; in all important things they do not need our teaching, while we may learn much from them. In one of the underground kitchens, I found an old woman who had been living there for twelve years. In spite of every obstacle, and in the midst of such surroundings as I have described, she was spotlessly clean, and had done the very best for the wretched place: the broken bars of the grate she had bound in their places with little bits of wire; the great rents in the wall, one of which went right through to the open air, she had stuffed with rags, the jagged ends of which she had actually taken the trouble to trim neatly with scissors; she had papered the walls, and as they were so damp that the paste was perpetually losing its hold, she patiently fastened up the long strips of paper fresh every week. With all this work for it, she had naturally become so fond of her little home that it nearly broke her heart to think of leaving it. So we determined not to tear her away from it. After a time, however, the force of our former arguments told upon her, and suddenly, one day, she volunteered to move. She has kept her new room, as one would expect, in a state of neatness and order that is quite perfect. She has since been growing less and less able to work, but she has always paid her rent, she has never asked for help, nor would she even accept the small boon of my lending her some money until she could give the due notice which would enable her to draw out her own savings from the bank where she had placed them. She has lived thirty-five years in London, a single woman depending entirely on herself, without parish allowance or other aid, and has had strength to keep up her standard of cleanliness and independence, and a spirit of patient trustfulness that is unfailing. Her life on earth is nearly over; she is now confined to her bed, for the most part quite alone, without even a bell to summon aid: yet there she lies in her snow-white bed as quietly as a little child settling itself to sleep, talking sometimes with a little pride of her long life's work, sometimes with tenderness of her old days in Ireland long ago, and saying gently that she does not wish to be better; she wants to go 'home'. Even in the extremity of her loneliness only a small mind could pity her. It is a life to watch with reverence and admiration.

We can rarely speak of the depths of the hearts we learn to know, or the lives we see in the course of our work. The people are our friends. But sometimes, when such as this old woman seem to have passed beyond us all, and to have entered into a quiet we cannot break, we may just glance at a life which, in its simplicity and faithfulness, might make the best of us ashamed.

Since we began our work in the court there has been a marked improvement in many of the people. I may just say, as examples, that the passionate Irish tenant, who locked me into her room, did not leave us, but has settled down happily, and has shown me more than one act of confidence and kindly feeling; that the old woman whose 'bits o' things' would look nothing if brought upstairs, after having been long in a light room, has now asked for a larger one, having freed herself from a debt which cramped her resources, and has begun to save; and that the two dark-eyed children were ultimately won over to trust in us. Their mother—a most degraded woman—when she at last appeared, proved to be living a very disreputable life, and the only hope for the children was to get them away from her influence. My first triumph was in getting the girl to exert herself enough to become one of our scrubbers; and finally, a year ago, we were able to persuade her to go to a little industrial school in the country, where she has since been joined by a sister of hers, who turned up subsequently to my first visits. Unfortunately the mother absconded, taking the boy with her, while we were still hoping to get him sent away to a training-school also; but, even in the short time that he remained with us, I had got some hold over him. By dint of making an agreement with him that I would myself fetch him at eight one morning, and help him to prepare his toilet so as to be fit for the nearest ragged school, I got him to begin learning; and when once the ice was broken, he went frequently of his own accord.

Opportunities for helping people at some important crisis of their lives not unfrequently present themselves. For instance, soon after we came into possession of the court, I once or twice received rent from a young girl, whom I generally found sitting sadly in a nearly bare room, holding in her arms a little baby. She looked so young that I thought at first the baby must be her sister, but it turned out to be her own child. Her husband seemed a mere boy, and was, in fact, only nineteen. One day, when the rent was not forthcoming, I learnt their story. It appeared that an aunt had promised the lad a sovereign to set him up as a costermonger, if he married the girl; but he had not bargained for prepayment, and the promise was not fulfilled. This marriage-portion, which was to have procured them a stock of herrings, had never been forthcoming. This seemed an occasion upon which a small loan might be of the utmost use. I accordingly lent them the much-needed sovereign (which they have since punctually repaid), and thus saved the young couple from being driven to the workhouse, and gave them a small start in life.

To show further the various opportunities afforded us by our footing with the people, I will describe one of our weekly collections of savings.

On Saturday evenings, about eight o'clock, the tenants know that we are to be found in the 'club-room' (one of the former shops of the court, and now used by us for a men's club, and for boys and girls' evening classes, as well as for this purpose of collecting savings), and that they may come to us there if they like, either for business or a friendly chat.

Picture a low, rather long room, one of my assistants and myself sitting in state, with pen and ink and bags for money, at a deal table under a flaring gasket; the door, which leads straight into the court, standing wide open. A bright red blind, drawn down over the broad window, prevents the passers-by from gazing in there, but round the open door there are gathered a set of wild, dirty faces looking in upon us. Such a semicircle they make, as the strong gas-light falls upon them! They are mostly children with dishevelled hair, and ragged, uncared-for clothes; but above them, now and then, one sees the haggard face of a woman hurrying to make her Saturday evening purchases, or the vacant stare of some half-drunken man. The grown-up people who stop to look in are usually strangers, for those who know us generally come in to us. 'Well! they've give it this time, anyhow', one woman will exclaim, sitting down on a bench near us, so engrossed in the question of whether she obtains a parish allowance that she thinks 'they' can mean no one but the Board of Guardians, and 'it' nothing but the much-desired allowance. 'Yes, I thought I'd come in and tell you', she will go on; 'I went up Tuesday—' And then will follow the whole story.

'Well, and how do you find yourself, Miss?' a big Irish labourer in a flannel jacket will say, entering afterwards; 'I just come in to say I shall be knocked off Monday; finished a job across the park: and if so be there's any little thing in whitewashing to do, why, I'll be glad to do it.'

'Presently', we reply, nodding to a thin, slight woman at the door. She has not spoken, but we know the meaning of that beseeching look. She wants us to go up and get her husband's rent from him before he goes out to spend more of it in drink.

The eager, watchful eyes of one of our little scrubbers next attract attention; there she stands, with her savings-card in her hand, waiting till we enter the sixpences she has earned from us during the week. 'How much have I got?' she says eyeing the written sixpences with delight, 'because mother says, please, I'm to draw out next Saturday; she's going to buy me a pair of boots.'

'Take two shillings on the card and four shillings rent', a proudly happy woman will say, as she lays down a piece of bright gold, a rare sight this in the court, but her husband has been in regular work for some little time.

'Please, Miss', says another woman, 'will you see and do something for Jane? She's that masterful since her father died, I can't do nothing with her, and she'll do no good in this court. Do see and get her a place somewheres away.'

A man will enter now: 'I'll leave you my rent tonight, Miss, instead o' Monday, please; it'll be safer with you than with me.'

A pale woman comes next, in great sorrow. Her husband, she tells us, has been arrested without cause. We believe this to be true; the man has always paid his way honestly, worked industriously, and lived decently. So my assistant goes round to the police-station at once to bail him, while I remain to collect the savings. 'Did he seem grateful?' I say to her on her return. 'He took it very quietly', is her answer; 'he seemed to feel it quite natural that we should help him.'

Such are some of the scenes on our savings' evenings; such some of the services we are called upon to render; such the kind of footing we are on with our tenants. An evening such as this assuredly shows that our footing has somewhat changed since those spent in this court during the first winter.

My readers will not imagine that I mean to imply that there are not still depths of evil remaining in this court. It would be impossible for such a place as I described it as being originally to be raised in two years to a satisfactory condition. But what I do contend is, that we have worked some very real reforms, and seen some very real results. I feel that it is in a very great degree a question of time, and that, now that we have got hold of the hearts of the people, the court is sure to improve steadily. It will pay as good a percentage to its owners, and will benefit its tenants as much as any of the other properties under my management have done. This court contains two out of eight properties on which the same plans have been tried, and all of them are increasingly prosperous. The first two were purchased by Mr Ruskin.

It appears to me then to be proved by practical experience, that when we can induce the rich to undertake the duties of landlord in poor neighbourhoods, and ensure a sufficient amount of the wise, personal supervision of educated and sympathetic people acting as their representatives, we achieve results which are not attainable in any other way. It is true that there are Dwellings' Improvement Societies, and the good these societies do is incalculable; I should be the last to underrate it. But it is almost impossible that any society could do much for such places as the court of which we have spoken, because it is there not so much a question of dealing with houses alone, as of dealing with houses in connection with their influence on the character and habits of the people who inhabit them. If any society had come there and put those houses into a state of perfect repair at once, it would have been of little use, because its work would have been undone again by the bad habits and carelessness of the people. If improvements were made on a large scale, and the people remained untouched, all would soon return to its former condition. You cannot deal with the people and their houses separately. The principle on which the whole work rests is that the inhabitants and their surroundings must be improved together. It has never yet failed to succeed.

Finally, I would call upon those who may possess cottage property in large towns, to consider the immense power they thus hold in their hands, and the large influence for good they may exercise by the wise use of that power. When they have to delegate it to others, let them take care to whom they commit it, and let them beware lest, through the widely prevailing system of sub-letting, this power ultimately abide with those who have neither the will nor the knowledge which would enable them to use it beneficially—with such as the London landladies described at the beginning of this paper. The management of details will seldom remain with the large owners, but they may choose at least trustworthy representatives, and retain at least as much control over their tenants, and as much interest in them, as is done by good landlords in the country.

And I would ask those who do *not* hold such property to consider whether they might not, by possessing themselves of some, confer lasting benefits on their poorer neighbours?

In these pages I have dwelt mainly on the way our management affects the people, as I have given elsewhere my experience as to financial matters and details of practical management. But I may here urge one thing on those about to undertake to deal with such property—the extreme importance of enforcing the punctual payment of rents. This principle is a vital one. Firstly, because it strikes one blow at the credit system, that curse of the poor; secondly, because it prevents large losses from bad debts, and prevents the tenant from believing he will be suffered to remain, whatever his conduct may be, resting that belief on his knowledge of the large sum that would be lost were he turned out; and, thirdly, because the mere fact that the man is kept up to his duty is a help to him, and increases his self-respect and hope of doing better.

I would also say to those who, in the carrying out of such an undertaking, are brought into immediate contact with the tenants, that its success will depend most of all on their giving sympathy to the tenants, and awakening confidence in them; but it will depend also in a great degree on their power of bestowing concentrated attention on small details.

For the work is one of detail. Looking back over the years as they pass, one sees a progress that is *not* small; but day after day the work is one of such small things, that if one did not look beyond and through them they would be trying—locks to be mended, notices to be served, the missing shillings of the week's rent to be called for three or four times, petty quarrels to be settled, small rebukes to be spoken, the same remonstrances to be made again and again.

But it is on these things and their faithful execution that the life of the whole matter depends, and by which steady progress is ensured. It is the small things of the world that colour the lives of those around us, and it is on persistent efforts to reform these that progress depends; and we may rest assured that they who see with greater eyes than ours have a due estimate of the service, and that if we did but perceive the mighty principles underlying these tiny things we should rather feel awed that we are entrusted with them at all, than scornful and impatient that they are no larger. What are we that we should ask for more than that God should let us work for Him among the tangible things which He created to be fair, and the human spirits which He redeemed to be pure? From time to time He lifts a veil and shows us, even while we struggle with imperfections here below, that towards which we are working—shows us how, by governing and ordering the tangible things one by one, we may make of this earth a fair dwelling-place; and far better still, how by cherishing human beings He will let us help Him in His work of building up temples meet for Him to dwell in—faint images of that best temple of all, which He promised that He would raise up on the third day, though men might destroy it.

4

Selections from Octavia Hill's
Letters to Fellow - Workers

A Crusade for the Poor

WÈ have been very happy in securing a great many fresh workers, who have come in most heartily to join in what we are doing. I think it is splendid to find so many and such earnest ones. Of course we want more. I suppose we always shall, for fresh work is ever opening out before us. Perhaps the place where I most feel workers needed now is for the Charity Organisation Society in the South of London. It is of the deepest import- ance that the Charity Organisation Society should not become a fresh relieving society, for added societies are an evil, and besides it can never investigate cases, and organise charities as it ought if it becomes a relief society. But the Charity Organisation Society must secure abundant and wise relief where needed, and it must stop that which is injurious. To accomplish these two ends it must win the confidence of private donors and relief agencies. Besides this if its investigations are to be trustworthy and effectual, and gently conducted, they must be watched over by people of education, and with deep sympathy with the poor. You cannot learn how to help a man, nor even get him to tell you

---

Octavia began having her letters to fellow-workers printed when the volume of correspondence with her various helpers and donors made the continuance of a personal corres- pondence impractical. Each letter gave an account of the principal activities for the previous year, and was followed by the annual accounts. The first printed letter covered 1872, the last 1911—the year before her death—and they appeared annually, with a very few exceptions. In spite of their growing popularity, Octavia resisted all attempts to persuade her to publish them.

what ails him till you care for him. For these reasons volunteers must rally round the Charity Organisation Society, and prevent it from becoming a dry, and because dry, an ineffectual machinery for enquiring about the people; volunteers must themselves take up the cases from the Committees, must win the co-operation of local clergy, and support them in the reform of their charities, must themselves superintend the agents, and conduct the correspondence, and for all this work we want gentlemen, specially for the poorer districts. Do you know what people tell me? That they don't expect to find honorary secretaries for the thirty-seven district committees willing to work steadily and who have time to spare! I know how many people there are busy all day, and I am thankful to think of it, for work is a happy, good thing, and when such people give of their not abundant leisure generously to the poor it is valuable in kind, for they bring to bear the power of trained workers, and the fervour of those who have sacrificed something to make their gift. But do you mean to tell me that among the hundreds who have no professional work, young men of rank or fortune, older men who have retired from active work, there are not thirty-seven in all this vast rich city who care enough for their poor neighbours to feel it a privilege to give a few hours twice or thrice weekly or even daily to serve them? My friends, I am sure that there are. The sense of the solemnity of life and its high responsibility is increasing among men, and the form it is taking is that of desiring to serve the poor. The same spirit which prompted men in another age to free the Holy Land, to found monasteries, to enter our own Church, now bids them work for men as men; for the poor first, as having nothing but their manhood to commend them to notice. 'Oh, yes', I am told, 'you will find gentlemen of leisure attend committees in the West, but the poor districts are too far out of the way.' Out of the way! Yes, so out of the way that we must set the need very distinctly before rich volunteers, or they will never come across it now that the poor and rich are so sadly divided into different neighbourhoods. But show them the need, and never fear the distance. What, a paltry three or four miles which they would walk before they began a day's shooting, and never count it in the day's work! What, the trouble of a short railway journey, and the annoyance of dirt and noise separate their poorer fellow citizens from those who, if there were a war and a cause they believed in, would meet danger and death in hideous forms without shrinking! The need is not before their bodily eyes, their imaginations are dim and indistinct, but let anyone they trust take them quietly for a few days face to face with the want, without exaggerating it, simply and silently, and if there are not thirty-seven men of leisure who will come forward, and work too, yes twice or thrice thirty-seven, then I don't know English hearts at all.

Whether they will find the problems very easy to deal with when they come face to face with them is another matter. But they must have patience, and realize that problems must be well looked into before they can be solved, and are not solved except by men resolved to grapple with difficulties one by one as they arise. How many of the thirty-seven will be wise enough or great enough to make themselves the centre of other workers I don't feel sure; but of their going, and of their working when once they see the want, I have no doubt.

Extract from the "Letter to My Fellow-Workers: Work Among the Poor During 1875"
****

The Need for More Workers

I have received, but just after my accounts were closed and ready for auditing, a very munificent donation, the account of which will appear in next year's letter. It opens before me larger vistas of possible money help to my friends hard at work among the poor than I ever began any year with before. While the thought of its administration fills me with joy, it fills me, too, with a sort of awe—for who am I that such power should be given me?—and I can only hope that I may be made humble and gentle, for in such a temper alone can the needs of the poor be made visible. The trust is like a call to me to tell me that you, my friends, those whom I know well and those I have never seen, look to me with confidence that I shall still be able to be your representative among the poor, however broken I have become during the late years, and your hope sometimes is a lesson to me to keep my own high, where no earthly mists can dim it. I think it right to mention this large gift, but I hope it will not make any of you, my old friends, think I do not need your help this year. I think I shall want it as much as ever, for this sum, being a large one, will probably be best spent on large objects, and the work I have had on hand for years should not suffer. Moreover, the mere fact of administering it will bring me face to face with much want, and for that I may need greater resources than are at my disposal. Send money then to me as of old, if you easily can, only remember *never* send it if it prevents your giving to any person or things you yourselves know and watch, and for which you are certain your gifts are helpful, for those gifts are best of all and thrice blessed.

In conclusion, I have but one subject more to refer to, and that is our great need of additional workers in our courts. The courts are numerous, the funds for their purchase are practically unlimited, but the quiet, steady, permanent workers, whom it is worth while to train, and who afterwards exercise an abiding influence in our courts, though they are increasing in number and very greatly in efficiency, are not by any means as numerous as they should be. During my absence every one has been buying courts, and so few, comparatively, have been training workers. I have now taken one to train myself, and one of my best friends, who is in daily communication with me, is ready to train another, and I would at all times be thankful to tell workers where they could serve a sort of apprenticeship. Surely there must be many volunteers who would care to take charge of some group of tenants, large or small, near their own quiet homes, or in some dreadful district of poverty, with the sort of quiet continuous control which may slowly mould the place and people to conformity with a better standard than prevails in poor courts in general. Surely there are some who would prefer the simple and natural relation to the poor which springs from mutual duties steadily fulfilled, to the ordinary intercourse between uncertain donors, and successive recipients of chance gifts. If any one should read this who would care to learn how to take a court and its occupants quietly in hand and establish such rule there as should be beneficial, if they come not with high hopes of gushing gratitude, of large, swift, visible result, but remembering the patience of the great husbandmen content to sow good seed and trust that in time it will bear fruit somehow, if they come ready to establish gradually such arrangements as must tell on the lives of their poorer neighbours, if they come with reverent spirits prepared to honour all that is honourable in the families they have charge of, and gradually to let the ties of real friendship grow up so that poor and rich may be friends as in a country parish, let them come to me and I will shew them work that I think they will feel opens to them a sphere of unnoticed usefulness such as few others can equal. Let them come quickly, for the need is great.

Extract from the "Letter to My Fellow-Workers: Work Among the Poor During 1881"
****

Resist the Temptation to Rebuild

We have a larger number of workers in training for management of houses than I have had for some years. Some of them shew promise of being soon capable of taking the lead in more respons- ible positions than they now occupy. I am consequently ready with their kind and increasing help, to take over two, or possibly three, more poor courts or blocks of buildings to manage for any owners caring for the people, who may wish to place them under my charge. I should prefer to take old houses, and should like them to be in a decidedly poor neighbourhood. I am sure old houses form much the best training ground for workers among the poor, besides which in them, inevitably, one can meet and help a lower class of people than in any new buildings, however cheaply they may be let. If a court is taken over full of its old inhabitants, there are some among them who have the opport- unity of being raised in and with it, who never could have such an opportunity in any new buildings. In letting to new tenants one must ask for good references; the drunkard, the dirty thriftless woman, is rarely accepted, cannot be accepted; the poor may indeed be received, but not those whose character is doubtful: the preference is fairly and rightly given to the sober, industrious and clean. But buy up, or take over, a court full of the less hopeful tenants, and it becomes your duty to try them; some of them always respond to the better influences, and are permanently raised. In old houses, moreover, unsatisfactory tenants can be tested much more easily, there is no risk of their destroying expensive appliances, they can be encouraged by the gradual improvement in proportion to their own care of the places they are in. In new houses nothing is to be gained by tenants by their care, for nothing is to be added, while much may be lost by their carelessness. In old houses the reverse is the case, the fresh distemper, the mended grate, the new cupboard, can be offered as a reward for care, while one or two more banisters broken or burnt are not a very serious loss to the landlord. Now though all classes of the poor want help of one kind or another, and the encouragement of the striving is perhaps *more* lost sight of just now than reform of the thriftless, yet the former is work which many are fitted to carry on; the latter must be done, if it is to be done at all, by some such agency as our own. Ladies must do it, for it is detailed work; ladies must do it, for it is household work; it needs, moreover, persistent patience, gentleness, hope. There is great need that someone should build quite simply for the very poor; it requires special experience to plan and manage such houses, still I do not purpose in the opening year to enter upon this work. The more personal one, I am satisfied, is even more pressing, it cannot be done except by some such group of workers as our own. The need of it is not clearly before the public yet; in all the late stir the cry has been as to the dreadfulness of the houses and the landlords. If all that is true under this head were remedied to-morrow, the public would see—clear sighted workers face to face with the poor *do* see—that a large class would remain, which could not, without education, be drafted into better houses. With that class we, if anyone, must deal, and I would earnestly ask those who are working with me not to lose sight of that fact, not to be led away by tempting plans for rebuilding, but to remember that singly the people must be dealt with, that face to face only can their education be carried on, that it will take years to accomplish, and many workers will be needed for it, and for the sake of London and our country time should not be lost; and that we, like our Master, must set ourselves to seek and save that which is lost.

I should wish our fresh courts then to be in a poor district, we have so much strength now that we ought to be face to face with a larger body of the poor once more. Two or three of my friends, who will themselves manage them, are willing to buy courts. I hope they will buy old ones rather than build new. For myself I feel rather doubtful as to whether, in the uncertainty as to public action, buying at all, just now, can be safely recommended to anyone who depends on receiving a fair interest for their capital;

and so, having now a pretty strong band of workers, I would rather manage for those who now own than recommend purchase to my friends; still, much might depend on the price, the neighbourhood, and the state of the houses.

A few words of thanks are due to those who have so kindly, and generously helped me with money. Taking into account the money sent me for Open Spaces, I never received so much in any year before. I have, besides, had a very great number of offers of money for houses. I have not been able to accept these as gifts, for I am firmly convinced that the people should pay for their houses. I have not been able to accept them either as shares, for a part of my own special work has been to connect individuals possessed of education, conscience and means, with particular courts in London. In this way has been established the relation between landlord and tenant, with all its mutual attachments and duties, as it exists in many country places. I have never, therefore, formed a joint-stock company for purchasing courts, but have got some one person to buy each group of houses. Some of the kind donors have allowed me to use their offered contributions for other purposes, to some I have replied that if a company is formed by men of practical experience to build simple houses for the very poor, I shall be delighted to put them into communication with the directors; at present, however, so far as I have heard, there is no company which is managed by those who have a full knowledge of the subject, and which has adopted sufficiently simple plans to suit the requirements of the very poor.

Extract from the 'Letter to My Fellow-Workers: Work Among the Poor During 1883"
****

The Cowardice of the Rich

It is two years since I have written to you, and I can no longer delay rendering an account of my stewardship, at least so far as the printing of my balance-sheets is concerned. I assure you they have been carefully and duly audited by my kind friend Mr Fletcher, though I did not think it well to print a letter last year. The truth is, I have been under a very strong conviction that silence was better in these days than any words. There seems such a rush of talk about work for the poor, so much self-consciousness forced on the doers of it, so ruthless a dragging to the light of all simple, neighbourly, quiet acts that would fain be done in silence as a natural and simple duty, that I felt as if it were really better not to write anything even privately to you, my old friends and fellow-workers. But I must print my balance-sheets in common duty of treasurer, and it seems unnatural to send them without a few words of thanks to all who have so generously and kindly helped me with money. Then, if I acknowledge the money, how can I be silent about the even greater help of faithful and continuous work? And then, how ungracious not to tell those of you who are far away in country places a little of the progress of the work with which you have helped! Besides, times change, and there may be things to say neither gossiping nor popular, which are hard to utter, and are not sure to bring any clamour of talk, being truths that the world would like to turn from, but which a low voice within says to me, 'Write or say, for those that will hear, who may not be so near the facts of life in a great city as you, and who will accept Truth though her beautiful face is veiled, and she looks sad and stern, but who know her as the daughter of God, and desire to see her, and ask for her guidance even if she leads them through ways they would not choose, but who trust, that where she leads, the paths are firm, if stony, and, though they are dark at first, must lead out into the sunlight and presence of God.' And the truth, so far as I see it, is, that the days are full of difficulty; the temper of the poor is difficult, the old submissive patience is passing away, and no sense of duty has taken its place; the talk is of rights, not right. The ideal the poor form for themselves is low, and the rich support them in it. The rich, on the other hand, while they are continually coming forward more and more to help the poor, are thoroughly cowardly about telling them any truth that is unpalatable, and know too little of them to meet them really as friends, and learn to be natural and brave with them. We have great relief funds and little manly friendship, idleness above and below, and an admiration for what is pleasant which degrades all life. This temper makes work difficult, and sometimes fills one with wondering awe about the future of rich and poor.

But, my friends, let us take heart. There is much work done thoroughly, and in God's sight, which will stand the fire and be proved as good pure gold. Wherever it exists, it tells in a quite marvellous way. One true-hearted clergyman, one conscientious mistress of a house, one firm mother who teaches her boy what duty means, one faithful workman, one human soul who looks day by day through earthly things clearly to the Lord of them, one statesman who is careless whether any follow or applaud, but who makes straight on for what is right, all of these prepare the way of the Lord, and do something to make England what we all wish her to be...

One distinct advance that is noticeable since I last wrote is the readiness shown by men of business and companies to place their houses under our care. A deeper sense of responsibility as to the conduct of them, a perception of how much in their management is done better by women, and, I hope, a confidence that we try faithfully, and succeed tolerably, in the effort to make them prosperous, have led to this result. This method of extending the area over which we have control has been a great help. It has occurred at a time when, owing to the altered condition of letting in London, I could no longer, with confidence, have recommended to those who are unacquainted with business, and who depend on receiving a fair return for their capital, to undertake now the responsibility of purchasing houses.

Extract from the "Letter to My Fellow-Workers: Work Among the Poor During 1884 & 1885"
****

The Advantages of Cottages

I mentioned in my last letter to you that the Ecclesiastical Commissioners were pulling down many of the old cottages in Southwark. I had been much impressed by the way in which the tenants cared for small cottages, and had noticed many reasons which amply justified their choice. I am aware that there are many well-managed blocks in London, but the arrangements for management in others are defective. In too many instances where numerous families reside, and the staircases, laundries and yards are used in common, they are under the supervision of one man, who is exposed to great temptation to overlook disorder. Even with the best will in the world, he is often powerless to enforce order, and to secure a good tone among the families in a large block. There is no organised system of government, except through him. The consequence is that if anything goes wrong, the quiet, steady tenants have no redress, they therefore leave, the rampant ones grow more unruly, good tenants avoid the place, which moreover through mismanagement has become insanitary. Empty places are tenfold more difficult to keep in order than those that are let, directors are in despair, the block stands half empty, while the neighbouring houses are over-crowded and there are ten or twelve applicants for any of them that fall vacant, but none for tenements in the block. Think what living in such close quarters must be, if there is no one to provide for the protection of the weak, or to consider and meet their wants. You get a family where the man works by night, he wants to sleep by day, the family in the next room are noisy and vigorous, there is no one to move him to the quiet corner of the block. Or there is a timid widow with little girls, she does not dare let them come up the noisy, ill-kept staircase, she wants to bring them up well, and the neighbours' children all use bad language. Think of the roughness and insolence of the drunken woman in the common laundry, of the dirt on the stairs when the tidy friend, or particular employer, comes to visit, of the drunken revel at night, echoing through the large building, and compare it with the quiet, separate little home in the cottage.

Then picture to yourself the utter impossibility in the block building of getting any kind of individual taste developed, such as the little separate yard allowed. Go down one of the courts of cottages which still linger in parts of London, pass through one of the passages and glance along the small back yards; in one you will see plants and creepers carefully trained, in another rabbits, in a third a little shed for wood, in a fourth all the laundry arrangements well provided, in a fifth the little delicate child sits out unmolested, in nearly all some evidence that the man has something to work at and improve when he comes home. The place has the capacity of being a home, not a couple of barrack-like rooms. If the court is well managed, the flags in front form a safe playground for the children living there among a small group of neighbours whom they know.

'Well!' you say, 'but is not the day for all this gone by? Land is too valuable in London for us to build cottages, we must have blocks.' Let that be granted for the moment, but that does not preclude those who own such cottages from keeping them where they are built. And I wish that any words of mine might avail with even one such owner, to induce him to pause and consider, very seriously, whether, at any rate for a time, he might not manage to drain, and improve water supply and roofs, and thoroughly clean such old buildings, instead of sweeping them away. As to cost, the cottages are far more valuable than the cleared space; as to health, they may be made, at a small cost, far more healthy than any but the very best constructed and best managed blocks. As to the life possible in them—of which the charitable and reforming and legislating bodies know so little—it is incomparably happier and better. Let us keep them while we can.

And suppose we grant that London is coming to block buildings, and must come to them; the preservation of the cottages gives time for the question of management to be studied and perfected. The improvement may come from the training and subsequent employment of ladies like my own fellow-workers, under the directors of large companies, and in conjunction with good resident superintendents. Or it may come by the steady improvement of the main body of the roughest tenants, making them gradually better fitted to use things in common. But, seeing in all classes how difficult it is to get anything cared for which is used in common, unless there be some machinery for its management, I think this latter remedy should rather be counted on as making the work easier, than as sufficient in itself.

While I am on this subject, may I remark that it would be well if those who build blocks would consider, in settling their plans, what machinery they are mainly trusting to for securing good order. If they depend on getting a small group of families with self-respect and self-control, who will take a pride in their separate staircase, they will build those staircases up straight from the street; but, if they are hoping to take in the rougher working people, let them plan the position and out-look of their superintendent's rooms, and bring the staircases down, say, to a common yard, the entrance to which their superintendent's rooms command.

In a rough neighbourhood this precaution may be needed, even if the tenants themselves are tidy, careful and trustworthy, for the police are not bound to watch private staircases, which, being used by many families, are apt to be open at night, and frequented by strangers with the worst results. Much trouble and expense may be saved by well considering these points before building. One advantage of bringing the staircases down into a large yard or playground is that the grown-up people, passing and repassing, are a protection to, and restraint upon, the children playing there.

Extract from the *"Letter to My Fellow-Workers: Work Among the Poor During 1886"*
****

The Need for Personal Involvement

I dealt last year with that portion of our Donation Fund which had been devoted to the sick, the old, the dying, or the helpless; not that spent in putting men or women into self-supporting positions, or in training the young for the battle of life, but that spent on the alleviation of pain, the comfort of those who will never work again. I said, and I feel it always, that this kind of help should have the very first place of honour in any scheme of Christian Charity. It is greatly to be impressed on almsgivers that the best way of helping the destitute is to find, if possible, some radical remedy for their destitution, such as training a widow's children: but that does not alter the great law that it is the helpless who are to be aided. Let us be clear therefore a certain portion of what we give should be just spent on the aged, the dying, and the disabled, not as if it were invested in preparation for life, but spent as in merciful help. But, oh! my friends, do not let us deceive ourselves. We may not enter into the blessing of thus sharing with the stricken-down people what God has given us of money, by subscribing to any huge, general, far-away scheme; we cannot delegate the duty, nor depute the responsibility on a large scale and without thought. If we are not prepared to give ourselves, at least to some extent, at least to the extent of choosing thoughtfully, watchfully, whom we will depute; and if those, who have not much time, but whose wealth claims from them large gifts, are not ready to choose large objects, so that the thought demanded may be possible to them; if they will not give in individual charity regularly and quietly, undertaking definite duty to groups of pensioners among the aged, or incurable, or to costly cases of training; and if they will not see that the personal care they cannot give is at least rendered by those whom they know and trust; then, believe me, their gifts are in terrible danger of doing harm. If we want to ease our consciences by giving money and yet will not take trouble about it; if we want to make a great effect with a little money; if we want to do what is popular; assuredly our alms will bring curses. The more I watch the more the action of the public puzzles me. By rashly pouring vast sums into new largely advertised, wholesale schemes, their feverish excitability is creating a body of thriftless, ungracious, mendicants, living always on the brink of starvation, because taught to look to what may turn up. And those who love and know the people have to stand sadly aside, feeling that all giving is fatal till such rushes be over; that growth of independence and thrift is impossible, while such wild action is frequent, and all the time they know that the blessing of quiet well thought out gifts to their friends among the poor is a reality; and that there are old men and old women who have saved, but whose club has failed; bread winners stricken down with sudden accident; incurable invalids, whom to know is a privilege, and to whom if we know and watch and adequately help them we are doing unmixed good. Neither the remedial, nor the incurable evils can ever be rightly met *en masse*. It is singly and by those who know the sufferers, that the right methods of starting them afresh, or the only safe granting of pensions, can be arranged. So we would ask for full, real, and due honour for the part of our work which is pure gift, and request help for it as being an undoubted blessing, bringing messages of peace and hope to many hearts. At the same time we would add that these gifts are only possible to us, because the members of our group of workers are in touch with hundreds of self-supporting homes, and know people before the time of loss or trial comes, or stand, as it were, beside them, sometimes for years, while it lasts. In our courts what we dread most for our people is the lavish and sudden rush of ill-considered gifts; and yet we would say there is a steady, quiet opportune gift which is the crown of all friendship and has a life-bringing blessing.

Extract from the "Letter to My Fellow-Workers:
Work Among the Poor During 1890"
****

5

Common Sense and the Dwellings of the Poor

*I*f in the midst of the excitement which has suddenly grown up with regard to the dwellings of the poor; if in the crowd of gigantic remedies which are suggested; if from visions of perfect homes such as one hopes may be realised some day, any one cares to turn to the consideration of measures of practical improvement which are now possible, and of steps which can immediately be taken towards the goal we all desire, this article may interest them. But it may be clearly stated at once that it embodies no scheme for suddenly providing perfect homes. Neither does it contemplate for a moment the disastrous policy of attempting to supply by the aid of the community a necessary of life (such as lodging is) for the working classes.

It seems dreadful to think that, with the public mind in a state of wild excitement, we may have schemes actually proposed which would be in effect to restore the old Poor Law system; to enable the improvident to throw the burden of his support upon the provident; by supplying houses at the cost of the public to tempt up to London a still larger number of migrants from the agricultural districts; and, what is worse, to undermine still further the dignified position of the working men of England, who have hitherto assumed that the support of their families was to depend on their labour, their self-control, their wisdom, and their thrift.

Moreover, a Government or municipality can pay for nothing except by levying taxes. The question therefore resolves itself into

First published in *The Nineteenth Century*, Vol. 14, December 1883, under the title 'Improvements Now Practicable'. It formed part of a symposium on working-class housing which appeared under the heading 'Common Sense and the Dwellings of the Poor'.

one of how the work will be best and most cheaply done. Almost all public bodies do things expensively; neither do they seem fitted to supply the various wants of numbers of people in a perceptive and economical way.

Working men may be sure that neither Government nor any other public body can take care of their children as they can themselves. The cost of all things must be paid and no payment brings so much effort as that rigidly demanded by the tax-gatherer, none gives so little pleasure in the result, for none meets less the various needs and desires of him who uses what is provided. Let working people fit themselves for better wages, and ask for them; let them go where work is plenty, and choose the work for which there is a demand; never let them accept a rate in aid of wages, whether in the form of houses, or of anything else. That which is supplied on a large scale gratu-itously, or partially so, rarely meets their wants. Contrast the medical relief given by the Poor Law, or even by the hospital, with that provided when men pay their own doctor or choose him from the staff of a provident dispensary. Contrast the workhouse dole with the wages earned, and then decide which is best; for, depend on it, both cannot be had. Whatever necessary of life is supplied under cost price on a large scale in the present state of the labour market in London will inevitably soon be deducted from wages.

Feeling sure that this is so, I dismiss all consideration of schemes which depend on sums voted by Government or municipality, except such as may still be required for sweeping away old abuses, that neither Government nor municipality ought to have allowed to grow up, and I will try to state what can now be done to improve the homes of the poor. I am by no means in the despondent frame of mind which seems to prevail just now, and I will endeavour to show, by figures generally known and accepted, that my hope is firmly based.

If heroic remedies are dismissed as unadvisable, no one can expect to immediately transfer families from homes such as those lately described in newspapers into ideal homes. For those to whom this thought is painful, there is this consolation: suppos-ing we could so arrange all outward things as to re-house them, the people themselves are not fit to be so moved, *and can only very gradually become so*. So vital a truth is this, so inextricably does it colour all schemes affecting them, that it ought to form the chief subject of any article now written; but, for the moment, the public is so entirely engrossed with the side of the question as it relates to houses, landlords, and rents, that it seems useless to dwell on it. Any one who cares to know what my experience on this subject has been, can see it in my little book, of which Macmillan is just bringing out a new edition. I only refer here to this branch of the subject to comfort those who, now the dark veil is lifted which hid from them the sight of the miserable homes which exist, long to think that at once these could be exchanged for such as they would like to see their poorer neighbours in.

But now suppose that, by waving a wand, you could suddenly arrange that all the families which you have pictured to yourself, as you read the newspaper descriptions, could have their homes thus far changed: that every foul drain should be put in order; that the old water-butts and neglected cisterns could be done away with, and the water-supply should be good, abundant, and easily accessible; that all those damp, dank kitchens should be emptied; that every room should be dry; that the tiny, fixed windows should give place to large ones opening top and bottom; that the rickety staircase up which you grope in the dark should widen itself, and become a firm, clean stone one; that the free air should blow up and down it; that every bit of rotten plaster and board should be made new; that the stifling wall blocking out light from the back rooms should be pushed back many a foot; and the narrower court in front widened; that you could give a common laundry to the tenants, and clear all the back yards of the dirty and crowded rooms which have been built out over them, and make the space into a playground for the children— that you could do all this without raising the tenants' rents a penny, nay, that you could probably reduce their rents 6d. or so a week. Would you care to do it?

I ask, because all this is possible now. Courts in various parts of London show it; balance sheets of buildings which have been thus altered show it; the figures quoted by Lord Salisbury with regard to the building societies show it. Would you care to do all this? I repeat; because, if you answer, 'No, not in the least, if I cannot give to every poor family three rooms each', then your problem is much more difficult. I will not say it is hopeless but will you not at least grant me that the one step is worth something, especially if I show you, as I hope to do, that it will not at all prevent your taking the second step whenever it seems possible? Only you must be careful to select plans for buildings in which the number of rooms taken may be settled from time to time as it seems best. I will explain what I mean presently. First let us deal with the question of cost.

I asked a large number of clergy and other workers in the East End the other day what rents they considered the unsanitary and worst rooms in their districts fetched. Some answered 3s., some answered 3s. 6d. I wanted to know what they would say: some people quote even higher rents. I should myself have said 3s. to 4s. for large rooms, or 2s. 6d. for small. The rooms which I know in model dwellings paying fair percentage—light, clean, dry, thoroughly healthy, with laundry and playground—rarely exceed 3s. and are very often cheaper. Surely as far as the financial problem is concerned there is no difficulty in entirely altering the whole character of the room and the house, and yet supplying the better article at the same price—might we not say at a less price? Take the figures quoted by Lord Salisbury. He says the Peabody Trustees supply rooms at an average of 4s. 4d. for two, that is 2s. 2d. for one. They, however, pay only 3 per cent; suppose we add one-third to the rental, which is more, of course, than would be needed to raise the percentage to 4 per cent, as this would increase the whole incomings by one-third, and the interest is only a part—I do not know how large a part—of their outgoings. That would raise the rental to 2s. 11d., a room, a lower rent than that of rooms in the terrible houses we hope to sweep away. But this rental may be still further reduced. The Peabody Trustees have spent, we are told, 75l. per room on buildings; while the Industrial Dwellings Co. have only required 51l. a room, and a block has been to my knowledge built by others lately at under 50l. per room. This reduces the cost by one-third, leaving a good margin for higher interest, or lower rental than 2s. 11d., whichever is deemed advisable. Again the Peabody Trustees have thought it well to build no shops. This restriction need not be followed by others. In central situations, and in those inhabited by numbers of the poor, such as the site cleared in Whitecross Street, the ground floors might have been utilised for warehouses or shops at high rental, which would have allowed the upper floors to be let at lower rental, or to raise the percentage, whichever may be thought best.

'Yes', say some of the objectors, 'but these results are obtained by those who build on land obtained under the Artisans' Dwellings Act, at heavy cost to the rates.'

Now, first, let us notice that the cost of that land has been enhanced by the expense of sweeping away old abuses, which are surely a very fair charge on the rates; secondly, that a part of the cost has been due to delay, and to cumbrous machinery. What would be thought of men of business who did as the Metropolitan Board of Works has, I believe done—declared that they could not consider what they were going to erect on the ground till it was cleared, and who, when it was cleared, left it a year or two vacant? Thirdly, let us remember that, in estimating the cost, no set-off is usually made for the immensely increased return from the rise in assessed value. Sir S. Waterlow says that on the Bethnal Green estate, on which they cleared away 166 houses, the rateable value of which had been 1,227*l.* a year, the buildings substituted would be rated at 9,500*l.* The capitalised income at twenty years' purchase amounts to 41,360*l.*, which is equal to the value of the land.* The same kind of increase would accrue in many sites cleared under the Act. It is true that the cost is thrown on the metropolitan rates, and the return comes to the local vestry; it, however, affects London ratepayers, and ought to be taken into account.

But, independently of the Artisans' Dwellings Act, land can be had at ordinary prices which allow of rooms being let at the prices quoted above. I have always rebuilt on land obtained in the open market, and have several rooms let at 2*s.*, and many at 2*s.* 9*d.* each, and these in blocks paying five per cent net interest on the capital. It will, however, be truly urged that though there are good rooms in model buildings of all kinds to be had at less than 3*s.* a room, yet they cannot be had singly. That appears to me the main point to dwell on now. Had the plans for buildings on sites cleared under the Artisans' Dwellings Act been made with separate rooms, instead of suites of passage rooms, the

---

*   See Annual Report of proceedings at half-yearly meeting
     of Industrial Dwellings Company, August 1880 (Octavia
     Hill's note).

complaint would not now be made that none of those displaced had been re-accommodated. On the contrary, *entirely avoiding overcrowding*, a very large proportion indeed of the very poor might have been admitted.* There are a great many large families in such a population, but every one has not a large family! And there is, so far as I know, in new buildings erected, hardly any accommodation for the small family that wants one room—the single room, as a rule, is built for widows or widowers. Again, no provision has been made for the numerous very poor families who have one son or daughter at work, who can pay for a second little room, but not for all the appliances usually placed in model tenements.

Great care should be taken to reduce the cost of building and maintenance, and to diminish chances of disease, especially if the intention is to try to house a more ignorant and destructive class of people, unaccustomed to the use of even simple appliances. These objects may be attained by not carrying the water and drains all over the building; these cannot be supervised so well unless they are more concentrated and more simply arranged than they usually are in model dwellings. The water should be on every floor, but not necessarily in every tenement. It is no hardship for tenants to carry water a few yards on a level passage or balcony. The closets should be on the stairs, and a vertical drain should descend from them, not going near any room.

There should be a large number of separate rooms. I have heard it urged against the construction of such rooms that it is unadvisable to perpetuate the homes consisting of single rooms; that every family ought to have two, and that we should aim at providing them. I most heartily agree; but it does not seem to me that the construction of blocks necessarily let in two- and three-roomed tenements is leading so straight to the desired end as the building of rooms which can be let separately, such as those drawn on the accompanying little plan (see p. 100). The

---

* I am dealing now with the question entirely as one of finance and of space; whether the habits of the people would have permitted landlords to admit them into decent houses is another matter, with which I do not propose to deal here (Octavia Hill's note).

two- and three-roomed tenements look hopelessly dear and unattainable to the labourer or costermonger; he never goes near them, but shrinks away into some back court or alley. But offer him one large room separable into compartments by curtains or screens, such as he has been accustomed to, with space for him to feel at ease and to gather in his friends, charge him the same rent as he has been used to pay, let him get at home there, and then, when first his boy or his girl, at about thirteen years old, goes to work, and he feels that a little more money is coming in weekly, urge him, as the very best thing he can do, to take a nice cheap little room next to his own and opening out of the same lobby, and you will find there is hardly one man out of twenty who will not take your advice, even if he has to give up a pot of beer or two, or give his children fewer pence for sweets on Sunday.

So, at least, I have found; every court I ever bought has been a one-roomed court, and many a happy, pleasant little one-roomed home I know now; but, for all that, I have few one-roomed tenements when I look round after some years of work. By experience in the old houses one learns how to build new ones to fit the poorer people.

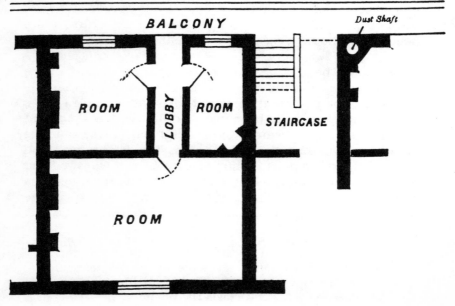

It will be noticed in looking at the little plan above that the important point is simple enough. A common stone-staircase leads to a balcony, from which little lobbies run. From each of these lobbies open three rooms. A family can take one, two, or three of these, as the tenant and landlord may agree. Depend on it, if houses were built like this, a great many poor would come into them. Again, it is a great point to make the rooms of different sizes. Whatever may be the case with the more well-to-do artisan, our labourers do not want a bedroom and sitting-room each of the same size: they want a comfortable-sized living-room, in which they live and sleep, and a much smaller room or rooms so soon as either son or daughter need separation. In one block we have even rooms at 1s. 3d, quite small, but invaluable, either to let with a larger room or for an old widow, light, airy, and with a fireplace, but quite tiny.

How cheaply rooms built in the way above described can be built must depend on many circumstances, in a great degree upon the care and economy used in building and management. It is clear from the figures quoted that they can be let even cheaper than the unsanitary rooms in back courts. My own opinion is that they could be let at a price which would enable a labourer to take a second room whenever his children began to grow up. One step on a thoroughly sound footing, and which did not involve any charitable or rate-supported scheme, would seem to me incomparably better than any which should begin the downward course to a rate in aid of wages. Depend on it, if blocks such as I describe were multiplied, if the existing laws for demolition were put in force, if sanitary inspection were stricter, the present difficulty would be to a large extent overcome.

It need hardly be pointed out that any suggestion of the possibility of schemes supported or assisted by public money entirely postpones any extension of that healthy independent action on the part of those societies or individuals who have helped the working people by meeting their wants on a remunerative basis. It will be impossible for those who cannot risk the possibility of their capital being wholly lost to embark any more of it in undertakings which may be suddenly rendered unremunerative by being undersold by rate- or State-supported buildings. And if any one should answer that these societies have hitherto done little for the very poor, it may be answered that it is not many years ago since the idea that building for artisans could be remunerative was scouted as chimerical. It was long treated as hopeless; then a few persons found out how such buildings could be made to pay; then many recognised it; now the ordinary builder knows it well. The same process has to be gone through before it is realised that houses for poorer tenants also will pay. A little patience, a little energy, conscientious economy as to detail, will prove it possible to provide for this class also on a remunerative footing. Only do not let those unaccustomed to the habits of the people sit at home and imagine what a poor man's family requires, but let experienced people supply the real needs first. The suite of rooms, the complication of drains, the expensive plan of carrying the water everywhere, the coal-cellar to hold a ton of coals, are some of them very nice: they are admirable for the mechanic who knows how to use them; they may be added in time, but they are not essential to health, they are costly, and they are not for a moment to be set in comparison with homes on an independent basis.

It is interesting to hear of the scheme for Sanitary Aid Committees. Their action might be helpful in getting vestries to put the Sanitary Acts in force with regard to large and small matters; but those gentlemen who can join the vestries themselves will be in a far more powerful and more recognised position. In order to overlook the smaller matters I hope the regular district-visitors may be encouraged to become the visitors for the Sanitary Aid Committees. It would seem unadvisable to create a new staff of visitors for a special object, seeing how many organisations are already working in the homes of the people, and how much better it is to have the inspection that of a friend naturally going in and out of the house. It is most important to give the existing visitors definite work, and to make use of their frequent visits. The poor are very naturally getting impatient of the numerous unattached visitors who go among them, unless, indeed, they are reconciled by the gift of shillings, a practise of all others the most demoralising. The sanitary visitor who only goes occasionally will, moreover, have no chance of keeping the tenants up to their own duties, which is certainly at least half the battle. It is important for visitors to remember, too, that whatever is said to tenants as to requirements from their landlords should be well within the law; tenants have a right to give up their rooms, or to stay there and to require that things which the law orders should be done, but they have no right to follow advice such as one visitor gave them, I see—that they should remain and not pay rent!

Sanitary Aid visitors, if they have tact and judgment, will be very useful, but they will find themselves in a much weaker position than those working in houses where they represent the landlord, who, therefore, can not only remonstrate with the tenant, or incite the vestry to action so far as the law allows it, but can in the last resort dismiss the tenant if his habits are persistently dirty or destructive—a power which rarely need be exercised, but is silently felt, whose duty takes them naturally into every room weekly, and who can order repairs or improvements when they deem fit. For the large number of courts not so cared for, the visits of sanitary aid visitors would be very valuable. But visitors would be incomparably more useful if they would train themselves to undertake the management of houses, and collect rent in them for a landlord—be he rich or poor, so that he be good—thus obtaining a regular position and getting to know their tenants well. It may be more difficult work: it will be much more thorough.

For in the long run it will be found, when this burst of excitement is over, that, without training these poorest people, no improvement in their houses will be of much avail. Read the most harrowing description of the worst courts, and notice how many of the sorrows would not be remedied by cheap, good houses; watch the people, and think what they would make of those good houses if they had them tomorrow; and then realise that the problem before you is far more difficult than the financial one; that it is more complicated than that of building; that you will have, before you can raise these very poorest, to help them to become better in themselves. Neither despair, nor hurry, but set to work with the steady purpose of one who knows that God is on his side, and that though He bids us work while it is called today, yet the great Husbandman is patient.

6

The Influence of Blocks of Flats
on Character

$\mathcal{A}$s has been said it is pretty clear that the working population of London is likely to be more and more housed in
'blocks', and it is not very profitable to spend time in considering
whether this is a fact to rejoice in or to deplore, except so far as
the consideration may enable us to see how far the advantages
of the change may be increased, or the drawbacks diminished.
The advantages of the change are very apparent and are apt to
appear overwhelming, and the disadvantages are apt to be
dismissed as either somewhat sentimental or inevitable.

The advantages may I think be briefly summed up under two
heads. It is supposed that better sanitary arrangements are
secured in blocks. It is also certain that all inspection and
regulation are easier in blocks; and on inspection and regulation
much of our modern legislation, much of our popular hope, is
based.

With regard to the sanitary arrangements I think all who are
at all conversant with the subject are beginning to be aware that
they may be at least as faulty in blocks as in smaller buildings—but it is undoubtedly true that even where this is so the
publicity of the block enables inspection to be carried out much
more easily and so, theoretically at least, a certain standard can
be better enforced. But this is not quite so true in actual practice
as those who put their faith in enforcement of sanitary law are

This chapter was Octavia Hill's contribution to the great
survey by Charles Booth *Life and Labour of the People in
London*, published in seventeen volumes between 1889 and
1901. Octavia Hill's essay appeared in the second volume
(1891) under the heading 'Blocks of Model Dwellings:
Influence on Character', pp. 262-69.

apt to imagine. Still it is true, and it is a very distinct advantage to be noted.

Your readers may be astonished that I do not put down the greater economy of the block system as a distinct gain, but I am not so wholly sure as many seem that it exists. For, first, room by room the block dwellings are not at all invariably cheaper than those in small houses. Moreover, I do not think we can permanently congratulate and pride ourselves upon, hardly that we can permit, a form of construction which admits so very little sunlight into lower floors, so that to the present cost of block buildings must, I think, be fairly added in the future such diminution of height or such increase of yard space as should allow of the freer entrance of air and light. This would increase the ground rent payable on each room. I think also that the cheapness of building many storey buildings is exaggerated. I have built very few blocks, but I have been consulted about some, and I have more than once proved in £.s.d. that cutting off a storey from the block as shown in the plans was a very small net loss, when cost of building, saving on rates, repairs, etc., and possibly even diminution in wall thickness justified by the lower elevation, were taken into account. We must also remember the increase of rent gladly paid by the sober and home-loving working man for ground floor rooms, lighter and pleasanter than if over-shadowed by higher blocks. I do not wish to generalise, the matter is one of £.s.d., but I say that the figures are well worth careful study on each building scheme, and that so far as the model dwellings are concerned I think their undue height in proportion to width of yard has sometimes been due to the mistaken zeal for accommodating numbers of families. I say mistaken, for with our increased means of cheap transit we should try to scatter rather than to concentrate our population, especially if the concentration has to be secured by dark lower rooms.

With regard to the disadvantages of blocks I think they may be divided into those which may be looked upon by those of us who are hopeful as probably transitory, and those which seem, so far as we can see, quite essential to the block system. The transitory ones are by far the most serious. They are those which depend on the enormously increased evil which grows up in a huge community of those who are undisciplined and untrained. They disappear with civilization, they are so far as I know entirely absent in large groups of blocks where the tenants are the quiet, respectable, working-class families, who, to use a phrase common in London, 'keep themselves to themselves', and whose well-ordered quiet little homes, behind their neat little doors with bright knockers, nicely supplied with well-chosen appliances, now begin to form groups where responsible respectable citizens live in cleanliness and order. What this life will be in the future will greatly affect London. Under rules they grow to think natural and reasonable, inspected and disciplined, every inhabitant registered and known, school board laws, sanitary laws, and laws of the landlord or company regularly enforced; every infectious case of illness instantly removed, all disinfecting done at public cost, it is a life of law, regular, a little monotonous, and not developing any great individuality, but consistent with happy home-life, and it promises to be the life of the respectable London working-man.

On the other hand, what life in blocks is to the less self-controlled hardly any words of mine are strong enough to describe, and it is abhorred accordingly by the tidy and striving wherever any—even a small number—of the undisciplined are admitted to blocks, or where—being admitted—there is not real living rule exercised. Regulations are of *no* avail, no public inspection can possibly for more than an hour or two secure order, no resident superintendent has at once conscience, nerve, and devotion, single-handed to stem the violence, the dirt, the noise, the quarrels; no body of public opinion on the part of the tenants themselves asserts itself, one by one disheartened the tidier ones depart, the rampant remain and prevail, and *often with a very fair show to the outsider* the block becomes a sort of pandemonium. No one who is not in and out day by day, or better still night after night, no one who does not watch the swift degradation of children belonging to tidy families, no one who does not know the terrorism exercised by the rough over the timid and industrious poor, no one who does not know the abuse of every appliance provided by the benevolent or speculative, but non-resident, landlord, can tell what life in blocks is where the population is low-class. Sinks and drains are stopped; yards provided for exercise must be closed because of misbehaviour; boys bathe in drinking water cisterns; wash-houses on staircases—or staircases themselves—become the nightly haunt of the vicious, the Sunday gambling places of boys; the yell of the drunkard echoes through the hollow passages; the stairs are blocked by dirty children—and the life of any decent hard-working family becomes intolerable.

The very same evils are nothing like as injurious where the families are more separate, so that while in smaller houses one can often try difficult tenants with real hope of their doing better, it is wholly impossible usually to try, or to train them, in blocks. The temptations are greater, the evils of relapse far greater. It is like taking a bad girl into a school.

Hence the enormous importance of keeping a large number of small houses *wherever it be possible* for the better training of the rowdy, and the protection of the quiet and gentle, and I would implore well-meaning landlords to pause before they clear away small houses and erect blocks with any idea of benefiting the poorer class of people. The change may be inevitable, it may have to come, but as they value the life of our poorer fellow-citizens, let them pause before they throw them into a corporate life for which they are *not* ready, and which will, so far as I can see, not train them to be ready for it. Let them either ask tidy working people they know, or learn for themselves, whether I am not right in saying that in the shabbiest little two-, four-, six-, or eight-roomed house, with all the water to carry upstairs, with one little w.c. in a tiny back yard, with perhaps one dustbin at the end of the court, and even perhaps with a dark little twisted staircase, there are not far happier, better, yes and *healthier* homes than in the blocks where lower-class people share and do *not* keep in order far better appliances.

And let them look the deeper into this in so far as our reformers who trust to inspection for all education, our would-be philanthropists or newspaper correspondents, who visit once a court or block, and think they have *seen* it, even our painstaking statisticians who catalogue what can be catalogued, are unable to deal with these facts. Those who know the life of the poor, know, those who watch the effect of letting to a given family a set of rooms in a block in a rough neighbourhood, or rooms in a small house in the same districts, know, those who remember how numerous are the kinds of people to whom they must refuse rooms in a block for their own sake, or that of others, know. To the noisy drunkard one must say, 'For the quiet people's sake, No'; to the weak drunkard one must say, 'You would get led away, No'; to the young widow with children one must say, 'Would you not be better in a small house where the resident landlady would see a little to the children?' thinking in one's heart also, 'and to you'; to the orphaned factory girl who would 'like to keep mother's home together', one feels a less public life safer; for the quiet family who care to bring up their children well, one fears the bad language and gambling on the stairs. For the strong and self-contained and self-reliant it may be all right, but the instinct of the others who cling on to the smaller houses is right for them.

For after all the 'home', the 'life' does not depend on the number of appliances, or even in any deep sense on the sanitary arrangements. I heard a working-man say once, with some coarseness but with much truth, 'Gentlemen think if they put a water-closet to every room they have made a home of it', and the remark often recurs to me for the element of truth there is in it, and there is more decency in many a tiny little cottage in Southwark, shabby as it may be, more family life in many a one room let to a family, than in many a populous block. And this is due to two causes, partly the comparative peace of the more separate home; it seems as if a certain amount of quiet and even of isolation make family-life and neighbourly kindness more possible. People become brutal in large numbers who are gentle when they are in smaller groups and know one another, and the life in a block only becomes possible when there is a deliberate isolation of the family, and a sense of duty with respect to all that is in common. The low-class people herd on the staircases and corrupt one another, where those a little higher would withdraw into their little sanctum. But in their own little houses, or as lodgers in a small house, the lower class people get the individual feeling and notice which often trains in humanity.

What the future will be for these wilder people I often wonder. It may be that some landlords will be wise enough to keep small houses standing for a time till the undisciplined are more trained; it may be that the gradual progress of educational and other influences may permeate their ranks and mould them orally as well as educationally (but of this I am not hopeful if they are herded together in blocks); it may be that some form of self-government, some committee of the tenants, may be arranged to organize and bring to bear the standard and rule of the better men and women (but it is difficult to think such an organization would be possible just where it is most needed, *i.e.* in the lower class blocks); it may be that more and more of such ladies as are helping me will be trained and enrolled by the directors or owners, and form a link between the tidy tenants and those who have control, a cheer and support to lonely resident caretakers, and a permeating influence for right and purity through the blocks.

Whatever be the way out of the difficulty, let us hope that it may come before great evil is done by the massing together of herds of untrained people, and by the ghastly abuse of staircases open all night, but not under police inspection, not easily inspected even if nominally so placed. The problem is one we ought all, so far as in us lies, to lay to heart, and do what we can to solve.

I have not dwelt here on what may be called the 'sentimental' objection to blocks, the purity of family life being recognised, even by those who trust most to inspection, as a necessity. But there is a sentimental objection which is felt by many to blocks. It is not confined to blocks for working people, though as their town home is their only home it affects them most. It arises, I think, mainly from two causes, the extreme difficulty, not to say impossibility, of giving to a block home that stamp of individuality which most other homes take from the life of the family that dwells in it, and the power of developing the individual life. The creepers in the back yard, the rabbits the boys feed, the canary the sickly child listens to, the shed for the man's tools, the washing arrangements, or the arbour, are all arranged to suit individual tastes, and for all these the separate house, or the small house, gives scope. In the block even the perambulator may be a difficulty, pets are impossible, even the nail for the funeral card or photograph of the son in Egypt, must be put, if at all, on the picture rail. The dweller in towns, however, must sacrifice much for the privileges he obtains, and he must accept the law of considering his neighbour rather by sacrifice of his individual joy, than by development of individual varied capacity. One feels the men thus trained may be meek, well-ordered, but will not be original nor all-round trained men. One can only note the danger and watch for any way of obviating it in some degree. The first sentimental objection to the block life is the small scope it gives for individual freedom. The second is its painful ugliness and uninterestingness in external look which is nearly connected with the first. For difference is at least interesting and amusing, monotony never. Let us hope that when we have secured our drainage, our cubic space of air, our water on every floor, we may have time to live in our homes, to think how to make them pretty, each in our own way, and to let the individual characteristics they take from our life in them be all good as well as healthy and beautiful, because all human work and life were surely meant to be like all Divine creations, lovely as well as good.

7

Municipal Housing for the Poor

$\mathcal{J}$HE newspapers are full of reports of speeches in which the words 'housing of the poor' occur frequently with reference to some municipal action. The borough councillors have been recently elected, and are evidently inclining towards some attempts in this direction. To crown all we hear on the eve of a London County Council election of a scheme upon which they propose to spend a million and a half in building suburban cottages, a form of building now being actively proceeded with by independent builders.

It would be well if councillors, candidates, and electors would pause and settle precisely what idea they have before them.

Are they desirous that municipalities or County Councils should house the entire working population, or only a certain proportion of them?

If the former, have they considered the magnitude of the problem, the numbers now in London, the numbers coming from the country, and the capital requisite? Do they think a local authority whose tenants are its constituents will be in a good position for managing well, for securing due payment of rent? Do they think the supervising body should be the judge of its own shortcomings? Do they think the conduct of huge business undertakings will tend to keep a public body clear from jobbery and corruption?

Or, take the other alternative. If it is assumed that the municipality will accommodate only a portion of the working

---

First published as 'Housing of the Poor', Letter to the Editor, *The Times*, 4 March 1901. The London County Council, created by Act of Parliament in 1888, had already become a major provider of social housing. The first council estate was the Boundary Street Estate in Shoreditch, begun in 1893, comprising 1,069 tenements for 5,100 people. The Millbank Estate, begun in 1897, accommodated 4,430 people.

population, not only will many of the above questions have to be answered, but in addition another. The remainder of the people will have, I presume, to be housed by private enterprise, and how will the municipal trading tell on that? How has the anticipation of it told already? Everyone who knows about the matter is aware that the good building companies and the good builders are not proceeding to meet the need of dwellings as they were doing before municipal action was talked of. Their work has been arrested. This is natural. When a public body which has the power of drawing on the rates goes into business no private person dares to embark in it. This is doubly true with regard to supplying houses which are themselves rated. House A belongs to a municipal authority which may fix its rents on the amount in desires to charge, not on the cost *plus* interest; it thus undercuts the private owner of house B. Not only this, it increases the rates levied on house B in order to supplement the insufficient rent received from house A. Under these circumstances the houses required which are not provided by the municipality will probably not be provided at all, especially as capital invested in building is tied up for a term of years.

Surely, therefore, it would be well for those who have influence in municipal bodies to pause before they thus paralyse independent building.

I hear people say, 'The need is far too great to be met by independent schemes, municipal action is essential'. I feel inclined to ask which agency they feel is the best able to meet a large and various need, the somewhat cumbersome, slow, costly, and stereotyped action of a public authority, or the manifold heads, hands, and hearts of a large number of individuals, such as the builders, who know local needs and are in touch with workmen's requirements, and responsible societies composed of thoughtful men gathered together to meet a public want on sound financial lines.

I believe that we ought to depend on independent enterprise for the supply of houses, while we look to the local bodies for the important work of carrying out clearance schemes, supervising building, and enforcing sanitary laws.

I am old enough to remember hearing from my grandfather, Dr Southwood Smith, accounts of the early struggles he was carrying on to prove sanitary conditions essential to health, and to establish at some risk of loss 'model dwellings'. Then came the time when we all knew that satisfactory houses under good management would pay, and countless good houses at reasonable rents were built. Numerous good societies grew up, never at any moment crippled for want of funds, and the whole problem was being well and rapidly dealt with. Paralysis, however, fell on the work so far as central London districts were concerned with the threat of municipal action. Withdraw that threat, encourage the many agencies again to build, improve means of communication, lighten, if possible, the burden of rates, and the need will in my estimation be gradually met in a satisfactory way, capable of variety and indefinite expansion.

8

Advice to Fellow-Workers in Edinburgh

*I*t is with the greatest pleasure that I have come here to meet those who are grappling with the same difficult problems that we have to face in London, to learn what, if any, differences there are in the problems, what steps you have found most effectual in solving them. Such a meeting of workers, aiming at the same objects, but pursuing them in different places, and perhaps different ways, ought to encourage us all, to make us more watchful and intelligent, more ready to learn from one another, and to sympathise with one another.

As this meeting happens to come at the end of my stay at Edinburgh, I shall before I read this have learnt, I hope, very much of the scope of your undertakings, of your special difficulties, of how you are meeting or have met them; but I write this in London before my visit. And that is perhaps as well, for it forces me to write about what may be interesting to you in our work, and the great principles which seem to me to underlie and govern all wise work among the poor, leaving aside minor points and local accidents to be discussed in detail with actual workers. What I am saying now will therefore have no special reference to

---

This chapter represents the text of a speech which Octavia gave to the Annual General Meeting of the Edinburgh Social Union on 21 November 1902. Set up by followers of Octavia Hill to provide working-class housing on her principles, the ESU became the first such body to take on the management of municipal housing, and by 1900 it was managing Edinburgh City Council's entire housing stock. However the ESU experienced the sort of political interference which Octavia warned would be the inevitable accomplice of municipal housing, and they withdrew from the arrangement with the City Council.

Edinburgh—on such questions I have no claim to speak— but my paper will contain thoughts suggested and facts ascertained during 38 years of London work.

If I begin with the difficulties I should say that most prominent among them is neither that of finance nor that of legal provisions. It is a moral one. It consists in the large number of untrained and undisciplined grown-up people who form the bulk of the prominent poor. I say the prominent poor, for I well know the steady artisan, intelligent and affectionate, who avails himself of better houses offered to him even if he has to make a sacrifice of creature comforts. I know also the patient industry of the quiet widow, who by the regularity of her small earnings, and her year-long self-denial in their expenditure, becomes one of our best tenants. I know of these, but these, I say, are not the prominent sufferers. They are apt to dip out of sight in silent, serviceable, often heroic lives, meeting their own difficulties with their own resources, becoming better men and women by doing so, and earning our respect and even gratitude.

The people who form the really difficult problem in all questions of housing, who give rise to ‘bitter cries’,* who attract the attention of the newspaper correspondent, who force themselves on the attention of the kindly but inexperienced charitable people are not these. They are the idle, the passionate, the badly controlled, the drunkard, the gambler, the beggar. I am not attempting to judge their guilt: they may have a thousand excuses, we might do far worse under their circumstances, our faults may be far worse in God's sight than theirs. I am only saying that they exist, and that they form the main difficulty in securing better housing—as well as in achieving many other desirable things.

As second among the housing difficulties I should place our own way, private, municipal, and political of dealing with these people.

To take the mistakes made by private people first. Many of us

---

*   *The Bitter Cry of Outcast London: An Enquiry into the Conditions of the Abject Poor* was a sensational pamphlet published anonymously by the London Congregational Union in October 1883. It called for state action to eliminate poverty.

are grossly ignorant of the temper of these people. We know too little of them to have any idea of their plausible lies, their out-of-sight debauch, their hopeless idleness. Some of us have an uneasy sense of the great advantages we ourselves have had, and we give with careless, or lavish, hand to ease our own feelings. And what is the effect of these ill-considered gifts? Of this misplaced indulgence? Believe me, you who have never watched its effect on the houses which it influences, it is deadly. It is the cause of a steady deterioration of character pitiable to watch. The drunkard is enabled to drink, the idle to idle and to bet. The uncertainty of the gifts upsets all attempt at plan; life becomes a lottery. Where do you think we find the least attempt at home life in London, and the most vice and drink? Not in the acres of poor houses in the entirely poor districts of East and South London, not in the darkest and most crowded courts, but in Notting Hill, close to the well-to-do classes. There the beggar is made and kept a beggar, there the public houses swarm with people spending their easily-got shillings, there the furnished lodging, paid for night by night, takes the place of the settled and thrifty house. The neighbourhood of the rich, the would-be charitable, makes the poverty which strikes the eye.

Take but one family under your care, watch its struggles, sympathise with its efforts, advise as to the health, education, preparation for work of its younger members, encourage thrift, stimulate the energy of those who compose it, and you shall see growth instead of deterioration, order succeed disorder, industry reap its quiet but sure reward.

Then take our municipalities. The existence of this undisci-plined class, seen by the superficial observer is driving corpora-tions to all manner of ill-considered, and to my mind, ill-judged schemes for housing. Such schemes are most unlikely to be financially sound. If they are not sound—even the expectation that they will not be so—is paralysing, has paralysed independent builders and thoughtful investors, so reducing the supply of good housing. Municipal building will probably degenerate into subsidising from the rates, open or concealed by clever balance sheets. This means rating the *really* poor, the steadily industri-ous, to meet part of the rent of their demoralised neighbours. Nor is the municipality ever likely to be a strong, or a wise landlord, using any helpfully restraining influence on the tenants. The tenants will be their constituents, their employees will be their constituents, and firm quiet beneficent rule which alone can help the undisciplined to grow, will be relaxed at recurring elections, even if it gets a chance of being established. To my mind too the municipality has its own great necessary function: that of overlooking—a function not exercised better for being itself a landlord.

Then turn to the political world. How we play with the great questions affecting the life of our poorest people! What cowardice is shown—or what ignorance—in questions affecting Poor Law administration, what hopes are raised about the old age pensions, without any considered scheme of granting them. Always the delusive hope raised, the energies paralysed, no vigorous effort to make our laws stimulate energy on which alone a man's happy future depends.

Now how do all these facts (which I assure you are most clear to me after long and close observation though I daresay many here may doubt about them), if they be facts, affect our action as managers of houses for the poor? I say as *managers* for to my mind it is as *managers*, even more than as providers, or builders, that our main usefulness lies. It is greatly and deeply true that more and better tenements are needed, but I would far rather see the present tenements left alone and the very best possible management of them secured, than I would see a multitude of new good tenements built and no good management established.

This house management is specially a task for ladies. It depends on watchful supervision with regard to detail, but it is none the less based on the great laws which govern good human life, called—somewhat dully—principles.

If any lady then comes forward to help in this your work of managing houses I would ask her, however small a share she means to take in it, what principles she proposes should guide her.

She is to be the head, not of one household as perhaps she is at her own house, but of several. What does she think will make her rule beneficent? She may learn a little by experience in her own house. She has been, perhaps, very anxious to make her household a training place, but she will have found that there are limits to the amount of reformatory work she can do there. She *may* be able to engage a cook who has been more or less addicted to drink, a young girl who has been guilty of a theft, or other wrongdoing, but she has felt that there must be a limit to what she ought to do in this respect, above all that, if she does anything, it must be at her own cost, not that of others. The erring member must on no account be a cause of dragging down others of the household, nor must she destroy the peace and comfort of the kitchen. The lady herself must give far more responsible supervision if she aims at this reformatory work. One thing moreover will become rapidly clear to her if she attempts it in her own house, and that is that her only hope of doing good will be not by 'overlooking' or tolerating the evil but by most serious action should it return. Quite as much for the sake of the wrongdoer as of others the tone will have to be 'such things cannot go on here, I am in charge here and I must not allow it'.

Now when any of you who have had such experience, or such hope of action, comes to be in charge of a sub-divided house, or a group of families, she will at once feel that the same principles must apply with even greater force. The fact that there are several households instead of one, that there are certain to be children to be influenced, that some of the residents may be in far greater temptation to which the wrongdoer has fallen a victim will make her responsibility ten-fold greater in deciding whether to retain or exclude an objectionable tenant. It will be in vain that kindly outsiders plead: 'what will become of him?' She will reply with sad seriousness: 'He must do better'. She will know that this is the only thing that can mend his position—or, what is more, his life. If she has that high gift of missionary power which can make him do better she will thank God for it, but she will know that mere toleration of wrong will not help him, and will corrupt or disturb others. She will feel that often the fact of having to move may be a lesson to him, and that if other landlords did the same it certainly might stop much evil, and that, be this as it may, she can no more leave him to go on doing definite wrong where she has control than she could leave wrongdoing to go on in a school.

I once heard a clergyman pleading with a friend of mine that she should keep as a tenant a man subject to attacks of *delirium tremens* and he urged that she should show Christian charity. She answered: 'It would be very easy and pleasant to me to say "yes" but you see it is not you or I that are kept awake at night by this man, and who have to get up all the same early to a long day's work. Ours would be cheap charity indeed, and hardly real'.

It may quite be that some of you in your own houses have come to the conclusion that you will do more good by keeping a healthy happy tone in kitchen and parlour making yours a household where mothers think it well for young daughters to live, and which radiate a good influence. Some on the other hand may exercise strong reforming power.

So it may be with your groups of tenants. Some of you may feel that to gather together and strengthen by association groups of really quiet families, giving them peace and order and good influences for their children, raising the standard of order, and securing a good environment for many who otherwise might fall into temptation is as good and useful a work as reformatory work. I have had both kinds of workers, and they have made the courts under their care very different according to their gifts, but of one thing I am sure: I have never had either kind of court usefully managed by anyone who was indulgently pitiful. The rule must be diligent, bracing, discriminating, and the sense of responsibility must be always heavy in deciding when order in the house and when the reform of the individual is the immediate duty.

I remember in the very first letter I wrote to Mr Ruskin when he thought of putting houses under my care I said I thought I could manage it if he did not want me to work with a committee. I could not do that, not only for want of time, but because the decision whom to keep and whom to send away must depend on hopes, beliefs, and perceptions one could not prove true to a committee. They might be right, or they might be wrong, but they would be the only basis for all attempts to make the people, or the places better. I was a mere girl then but time has only confirmed me in the view that whatever rules and committees may do for well-regulated families, it is personal rule and personal influence only which can raise the lowest, and time has increased with ever greater force my sense of the injury done by tolerance of wrongdoing, and the helpfulness of wise, strict government.

Take for instance the question of irregular payments about which leniency is so often urged. What do you do, I am often asked, when people can't pay their rent. If tenants tell me they can't pay it I ask them why, and if it be so I tell them to talk it over with their husbands and tell me what they propose, point out to them that of course credit cannot go on, and get them to do at once whatever they would have to do much later. But of course the time to meet such difficulties is before they arrive, by getting sobriety, industry, thrift, before the day of trouble comes. And what a blessing it is to the people to be out of debt. We hardly ever have to send away a tenant for non-payment—it is the rarest thing in the world. Once, when we did, the woman came back after some time and implored to be taken back again. She pleaded that it had been such a great help to her to have a strict landlady. And once when I was talking to a working man about our absolute determination to insist on regular payments, I expected him to make exceptions, or plead that it was hard, and he looked very grave and then said: 'Yes, I know it is best. You see they do say money is the root of all evil, but I often think credit beats it'.

Well, if you get all this well into your heads and hearts, and in very deed believe that your subtlest work is by no means ameliorating the outward condition of your people, but making them better, and that you will do this by helping their weak wills to do what they know to be right, you will not feel much difficulty about the more tangible part of the business.

There is much to learn, much that is technical to learn, about repairs, and accounts, and prices, and rates and taxes, and legal matters but they are definite and soluble under good advice. The more you help your tenants do their duty, the more you will feel it incumbent on you to be most perfect in fulfilment of yours. Not only must you be prompt, thorough and diligent but most gentle, patient and just.

As time goes on you will see your old houses steadily improve, yards encumbered with buildings will be cleared for playgrounds, windows will be broken out on dark staircases, lamps will lighten and so purify dark entrances, fresh cupboards, more cooking ranges will be added, perhaps a tree or two or many Virginia creepers may bring a memory of the country to out-of-the-way courts. Or if you manage blocks you may bring order out of chaos, cleanliness out of dirt, helpful co-operation and mutual confidence where quarrelling raged before. Anyway you will have near you a group of poorer friends whom you know, respect, and love, who have duties to you as you have to them, who meet you in a natural, independent, and friendly way. You will have watched them as you do your friends in another sphere through years of natural intercourse, and should death, sickness or sorrow come upon them you will be beside them as a real friend, and if tangible help is needed it will be only such as will re-establish right living and not undermine self-reliance and energy.

Do not be discouraged if sometimes you have to do a difficult thing, which seems a little hard to your richer friends, or even to your poorer ones, though the latter more often see its wisdom or necessity. Live to your own conscience; be sure that you have 'considered' the poor; qualify yourself for judging by patient, earnest watchfulness of a few; do not live to reproach yourself for having been among those who with easy, superficial sight palliate the immediate physical need by corrupting the human spirit in those who are meant to reach the stature of men and women. Look upon the body as the training place for the soul.

Remember that as Mr Browning tells us:

It takes the ideal to blow a hair's breadth off the actual;
It takes a high-souled man to lead the masses even to a cleaner sty.

In all humility, never despising the duty of attending to the merest detail about lock or tap which adds to comfort or perfection of outward things, but looking to the houses under your care as schools for noble living, and houses for happy families, exercise in hope, love and prayer the power entrusted to you.

9

Housing Difficulties:
Management versus Re-construction

---

*M*AY I address a few words to your readers on the housing problem, in order to draw attention to the fact that in many cases the evils in particular areas do not call for re-construction, but for wise and firm management? It is important to realise this fact, because there is a danger that small houses may be swept away in the desire for rebuilding where rebuilding is not called for. In such small houses the poorer tenants can be accommodated at low rents which are impossible after large building expenses have been incurred. Moreover, such houses are far better fitted for the less-disciplined tenants than block buildings. It is these less-disciplined people who form the main difficulty in the problem.

Perhaps I may best illustrate this point by reference to the district of Notting-dale, frequently mentioned in the press of late, and where we are ourselves at work.

Four years ago a friend purchased the leases of seventeen houses in a street there and put them under our care. We found them in the hands of middlemen, who let them in furnished rooms, often by the night, to tenants whose references could not be taken up; and the standard of cleanliness, order, and morality was what we might expect, and what has been mentioned in the press. It was this class of trade, and this system of no-management in the hands of ignorant middlemen, which produced the

---

First published in the Daily Chronicle, 1904(?). Published in pamphlet form and referred to by Octavia Hill in her letter to the fellow-workers for 1904. Octavia's involvement in the Notting Hill area began in 1899 when a clergyman asked her to manage five houses adjoining the church hall. By 1910 there were about 100 houses in the area under her control.

state of things described, and which obliged Mr Charles Booth to depict the area by a black patch amid the large spaces of red and yellow that mark the homes of the well-to-do.* A second cause of the deterioration of the dwellers there was precisely the neighbourhood of these very people designated as 'well-to-do'; but who, as a rule, are so very ignorant of the effect of their action on their neighbours as to scatter among them indiscriminate and uncertain gifts.

It was not the state of the houses which had caused the evil. The street is very wide and airy, and is composed of nice little six-roomed houses with good yards at the back. The sanitary authorities had kept up the appliances well, and had insisted on frequent cleansing; so that, though the place was swarming with vermin and polluted by its inhabitants, we found comparatively little to do in structural alterations. In fact, I feel that the houses lend themselves particularly well to just the work which will gradually raise this class of tenant, and which meets their needs.

Our first duty was to remove the middlemen and to enter into direct relations with the tenants. We introduced as managers, coming into almost daily communication with the tenants, a group of educated and high-principled ladies. The dirty furniture was removed, and the people were encouraged to provide their own. In this way, the rent being lower for unfurnished rooms, families could take two rooms for the same rent as one, thus mitigating the crowding. The closets, wash-houses, and yards were supervised; the drunken and rowdy inmates were, in a measure, both influenced and restrained, and the quiet poor were protected, encouraged, and gradually raised to better conditions. These small houses with rooms light and good-sized as things go, and which can be let to a small number of tenants with wash-house and yard in common, lend themselves well to the class of tenants most difficult to raise and provide for. No large expenditure in building has been incurred.

Rebuilding almost necessarily involves smaller rooms and higher rents. The floors of two rooms are let at 5s. to 6s., and there are a few small rooms to let at 1s. 6d. Three or four families

---

*   Charles Booth's great survey *Life and Labour of the People in London* was published in 17 volumes between 1889 and 1902.

who are set on quiet, are able to occupy a house and are not forced into contact, as in a block, with a number of less self-controlled neighbours; yet the fact that there are three or four in a house using yard, wash-house, and staircase in common, makes an excellent reason for that personal supervision so essential to order and cleanliness which we ladies are able and glad to provide.

Rebuilding is quick, clearance is quick; but this individual and detailed work necessarily takes time; nor is its effect easily discerned when looked at by the cursory visitor or newspaper reporter.

In my experience it is thus individually and gradually that this class of tenant can be raised; and among the means for their improvement I should rank as among the most potent the silent influence of those quiet and righteous families among themselves who can be protected and encouraged to live near them.

I quite accept the descriptions given of much that goes on in the street. I should be the last to palliate the sense of horror and shame that such things should exist among us; my own fellow-workers often come back awed by the weight of evil there: but I would point out that it is not, in this neighbourhood, the houses which are in fault, but the government of them and the lives of the inhabitants.

May I add a few words as to the measures needed to carry such reforms further?

The control of seventeen houses in a long street does not entirely secure order in the street, and though we have been able through the help of friends to add during the last four years nine more to the original seventeen, and to purchase eighteen at the further end also, which were not so bad, but were likely to become so, there remain many over which we have no control whatever. These are centres of disorder, and tell heavily against those we manage. The first point in any effort for further reform would be to get control of these. The short leases form one element of difficulty, and the ground landlords should be approached.

The law affecting the management of the public-houses in the district should be enforced. Evidence as to the conduct of these should be obtained and acted on. Indiscriminate giving should be avoided, and wiser action taken by the charitable. These people are not poor as a rule; they spend enormously in drink; they pay double rent, if it be exacted nightly, rather than half the amount if they have to keep it for a week; the men often will not work, but live upon their wives. All this is perpetuated by foolish alms-giving. I am working in South London, far from the well-to-do, and I do not find there nearly as many thriftless, shiftless people, nor one-tenth as many lying drunk on their doorsteps on a Bank Holiday, as I find when I go to Notting-dale. This is a heavy responsibility for the donors to beggars and impostors.

It is inadvisable to stigmatise a neighbourhood with such names as 'Modern Avernus'. The drunkards and the fighters are much in evidence; it is they who make the impression if you enter the street on a Saturday night; but in the houses them-selves, out of sight and quiet, are respectable little homes, gentle and industrious widows supporting their families, unobtrusive men returning to happy, well-conducted homes; and everywhere about among them managers set on their encouragement and protection, eager to give them extra appliances, or start children in good work, determined to secure decency and order for them.

I do not wish to praise these ladies; they are the last to desire it; they feel such work their duty; but I do say that it is by such influences in such a street, by such detailed supervision by those representing the owners, that such a group of rowdy people in the district in which they dwell can, so far as my experience goes, alone be redeemed and set in order.

Notes

1 In 1858 Octavia had contrasted her 'human work' with her 'artistic work' to which 'I feel sure more and more of my life will be called'. Quoted in Moberly Bell, E., *Octavia Hill: A Biography*, London: Constable, 1942, p. 72.

2 Quoted in Darley, G., *Octavia Hill: A Life*, London: Constable, 1990, p. 76.

3 Quoted in Darley, G., *ibid*, p. 38.

4 Quoted in Darley, G., *ibid*, p. 63.

5 Quoted in Darley, G., *ibid*, p. 73.

6 Letter to Mrs William Shaen, quoted in Darley, G., *ibid*, p. 91.

7 Quoted in Moberly Bell, E., *Octavia Hill: A Biography*, London: Constable, 1942, p. 75.

8 The Census of 1861 had listed 37 inhabitants living in eight rooms at No. 3, each room being treated as a separate household or unit of accommodation. No. 1 was divided into 11 units. As the house only had eight rooms, including the cellars, some of the rooms must have been sub-divided to make more than one unit.

9 From an article written by Lord Salisbury for the *National Review* in 1883, quoted in Darley, G., *op. cit.*, p. 225.

10 *Royal Commission on the Housing of the Working Classes*, PP 1884-5, XXX, 8864, 8866 and 8934. Octavia gave her evidence on 9 May 1884.

11 Hill, O., 'Management of Houses for the Poor', *Charity Organisation Review*, January 1899, No. 25, new series, p. 21.

12 As the news of Octavia's method spread she received many requests from interested parties who wanted to be shown around her properties. She refused absolutely to take any visitors around unless it was her day for collecting rents, as she regarded it as unacceptable to disrupt the lives of the tenants.

13 According to the Hon. Mrs Maclaglan, who wrote an account of her years spent as one of Octavia's helpers in Barrett's Court: '...in theory Miss Hill never allowed arrears for more than a fortnight without threatening, or a month without putting in the broker, but like many theories, hers were not always put into practice and I have known tenants in arrears for as much as eleven weeks. Probably she knew that they had a good deposit in the Penny Bank which she, or one of her chief workers, always managed in person'. [Quoted in Darley, G., *op. cit.*, pp. 134-5.]

14 'One cannot retain tenants living in vice, irregular in their payments, or violent in their habits.' Extract from the Letter to Fellow-Workers for 1906.

15 *Royal Commission on the Housing of the Working Classes, op. cit.*, 8866.

16 In 1880, 15 years after Octavia had taken on the management of Paradise Place, one of the tenants described it to Octavia's mother as '...so quiet now; there are such nice respectable people. We are all so comfortable here.' [Quoted in Darley, G., *op. cit.*, p. 208.]

17 Octavia's successful management of these large estates is reflected in a brief mention in the Church of England's famous report *Faith in the City*: '[T]he Octavia Hill Estates ...provide low-rent housing, responsibly managed. The sense of community among the tenants was encouraging. The Octavia Hill Estates offer a good combination of social benefit and financial return.' [*Faith in the City: A Call for Action by Church and Nation*, The Report of the Archbishop of Canterbury's Commission on Urban Priority Areas, London: Church House Publishing, 1985, p. 260.]

18 *Royal Commission on the Housing of the Working Classes, op. cit.*, 9134, 9135, 9136, 9138, 9144.

19 For example, Samuel and Henrietta Barnett, who had both worked with Octavia when they lived in Marylebone, had by this time moved to Toynbee Hall in Whitechapel where they had started the East End Dwellings Company.

20 The estimate was made by Miss Jeffrey, who worked with Octavia in the last year of her life. Jeffrey, M.M., *House Property and Estate Management on Octavia Hill lines*, Occasional paper no 12, fifth series, London: Charity

Organisation Society, 1929, p. 1, quoted in Brion, M., *Women in the Housing Service*, London: Routledge, 1995, p. 12.

21 See e.g. Jordan, W.K., *Philanthropy in England 1480-1660: A Study of the Changing Pattern of English Social Aspirations*, London: George Allen and Unwin, 1959; and Owen, D., *English Philanthropy 1660-1960*, Cambridge, MA: Harvard University Press, 1965.

22 Quoted in Tarn, J.N., *Five Per Cent Philanthropy: An Account of Housing in Urban Areas Between 1840 and 1914*, Cambridge: Cambridge University Press, 1973, p. 22.

23 The Metropolitan Association limited its dividend to five per cent and the SICLC to four per cent, but they did not always reach even these modest targets. Angela Burdett-Coutts built Columbia Square in Bethnal Green (1862) entirely at her own expense and only received a return of two per cent. She was not concerned, as it was a philanthropic venture, but such returns ensured that model housing would remain firmly within the philanthropic sector. In 1862 Henry Roberts, the architect to the SICLC who became an expert on working-class housing, came to the conclusion that, with great care and with expert knowledge it might be possible to obtain 3.5 - 4 per cent return on investment (Tarn, *op. cit.*, p. 43). This makes it all the more remarkable that Octavia was able to pay the owners of the properties she managed a dividend of five per cent almost until the end of her life, and this was in spite of the fact that she was dealing with the most destructive class of tenants.

24 *Builder*, Vol. XXVII, 1867, p. 99, quoted in Tarn, *op. cit.*, p. 62.

25 They are still standing, in good condition, and are now administered by the Peabody Trust.

26 Prince Albert had used his position as President of the Commissioners for the Great Exhibition in Hyde Park in 1851 to obtain permission (previously refused) for the Society for Improving the Conditions of the Labouring Classes (of which he was also President) to erect their model cottages in the grounds of Hyde Park. As a result they have always been known as the Prince Consort's Model Cottages, and there is a popular misconception that he designed them.

27 See Tarn, J.N., *op. cit.*, p. 24.

28 Quoted in Parker, F., *George Peabody: A Biography*, Nashville: Vanderbilt Press, 1995, p. 150.

29 From the founding letter sent by Peabody to his first Trustees, held in the archives of the Peabody Donation Fund and quoted in Tarn, J.N., 'The Peabody Donation Fund: The Role of a Housing Society in the Nineteenth Century', *Victorian Studies*, Vol. X, No. 1, September 1966, p. 10.

30 Peabody once summed up his philanthropy thus: 'I have not sought to relieve pauperism, but to prevent it'. [Curry,J.L.M., *A Brief Sketch of George Peabody and a History of the Peabody Education Fund Through Thirty Years*, John Wilson and Son, 1898, republished New York: Negro University Press, 1969, p. 15.]

31 When Octavia was giving evidence to the Royal Commission in 1884 she was asked: '...your work is mainly to reclaim the tenants that nobody else will touch?' Her reply was: 'Yes, the tenants and the houses, one might almost say'. *Op. cit.*, 9119.

32 The housing societies themselves entered into the spirit of the Act with such enthusiasm that they actually housed more people than had been on the sites before. The sixteen sites dealt with the Board of Works under the Cross Act covered 42 acres and had housed 23,188 people. After re-building they housed 27,780. Population density increased from 540 people to 660 per acre. [London County Council, *The Housing Question in London 1885-1900*, (ed. Stewart, C.J.) 1900, pp. 296-97 and appendix C, quoted in Tarn, *Five Per Cent Philanthropy, op. cit.*, p. 83.]

33 The Peabody Trustees bought seven complete sites, plus parts of two others.

34 The final price paid for the Whitechapel site was only half the reserve price placed upon it when it went to auction—but there had been no bidders. [Tarn, 'The Peabody Donation Fund', *op. cit.*, p. 27.] The overall loss to the Board of Works on all schemes covered by the Cross Act was £1,323,415 [L.C.C. *The Housing Question in London, op. cit.*].

35 Octavia, with her keen nose for subsidy, spotted it but, surprisingly, did not object. She argued that slums were like slavery: an abuse which society had allowed to grow up, and

which society would have to pay to put right. [See p. 95, also *Royal Commission on the Housing of the Working Classes, op. cit.*, 9092.]

36 Parker, F., *op. cit.*, p. 128.

37 Tarn, J.N., 'The Peabody Donation Fund', *op. cit.*, p. 35.

38 Prince Albert was President of the Society for Improving the Condition of the Labouring Classes and keenly interested in anything which improved the lot of the poor. In 1852 the Windsor Royal Society for Improving the Condition of the Working Classes was founded under the patronage of the Queen and the Prince Consort, and erected a row of cottages in Windsor Great Park. The Prince of Wales (later Edward VII) was a member of the Royal Commission on the Housing of the Working Classes, and attended on 16 of the 39 days on which evidence was taken from witnesses. He had supported Gladstone in the view that Octavia Hill should have been invited to become a member of the Commission. [Prochaska, F., *Royal Bounty: The Making of a Welfare Monarchy*, London: Yale University Press, 1995, p. 122.]

39 House of Lords, *Hansard*, 'Housing of the Working Classes', 22 February 1884, clm 1680.

40 *Royal Commission on the Housing of the Working Classes, op. cit.*, 8871.

41 *Royal Commission on the Housing of the Working Classes, op. cit.*, 8877.

42 *The Private Rented Housing Sector*, House of Commons Environment Committee, HC40, London: HMSO, July 1982, Vol. II, p. 170, cited in Minford, P., *et al.*, *The Housing Morass: Regulation, Immobility and Unemployment*, Hobart Paperback 25, London: Institute of Economic Affairs, 1987, p. 30.

43 *Social Trends 26*, London: HMSO, 1996, Table 10.16, p. 183.

44 Octavia was one of the first of the Victorian philanthropists to suffer the back-handed compliment of being credited with ushering in the welfare state. According to Canon Scott Holland: 'The voluntary effort that first discovered, by grave experiment, the true nature of the remedy, has, then, by virtue of its very success, to see its work passed on to the official system which alone is wide enough to cover the

ground. That is why Miss Hill's work has lost a little of its special interest. It had proved its case. It had converted the world.' [Holland, H.S., *A Bundle of Memories*, 1915, pp. 280-81.

45 Tarn, 'The Peabody Donation Fund', *op. cit.*, p. 20, n.

46 Daunton, M.J., *A Property-Owning Democracy: Housing in Britain*, London: Faber and Faber, 1987, pp. 40-41.

47 Tarn, *Five Per Cent Philanthropy*, *op. cit.*, p. 58.

48 *Ibid.*, pp. 85-87.

49 Oscar Wilde made a more serious contribution to the debate on character versus environment in the December 1887 edition of the magazine *Woman's World*: 'The poor are not to be fed upon facts. Even Shakespeare and the Pyramids are not sufficient; nor is there much use in giving them the results of culture, unless we also give them those conditions under which culture can be realised. In these cold, crowded cities of the North, the proper basis for morals... is to be found in architecture, not in books.' I am indebted to Merlin Holland, Oscar Wilde's grandson, for drawing this to my attention.

50 Quoted in Bradley, I.C., *Enlightened Entrepreneurs*, London: Weidenfeld and Nicholson, 1987, p. 51.

51 *Royal Commission on the Housing of the Working Classes*, *op. cit.*, 9193-9194.

52 When Octavia was working with Robert Hunter on drawing up the National Trust's memorandum of association she sought advice on the American movement to preserve open spaces from Ellen Chase, who had been one of her housing managers before moving back to the USA. Yellowstone had been established as the world's first national park in 1872, and there were other bodies set up in the USA to acquire and preserve land. However they were all public bodies, run by departments of national or local government. The National Trust, by contrast, was an independent charity, and, in the words of its historian Jennifer Jenkins: 'has proved well suited to the British wariness of state intervention'. ['The Roots of the National Trust', *History Today*, Vol. 45, January 1995, pp. 3-7.] As Octavia put it in one of the Letters to Fellow-Workers: 'It is a principle of modern life in free countries that we are not directed from above, as a tool, but

have to think out what is best to do, each in his own office'
[quoted in Moberley Bell, E., *op. cit.*, p. 122].

53 The Charities Aid Foundation's survey *Dimensions of the
Voluntary Sector* put the National Trust at the top of its list
of fundraising charities in 1993 and 1995, and in second
place (to Oxfam) in 1996 with a voluntary income of over £77
million.

54 See Jenkins, J., *From Acorn to Oak Tree*, London:
Macmillans, 1994.

55 The National Trust, *Facts and Figures Compendium*,
February 1997.

56 Address to Newnham College students, March 1898 [Ouvry
papers], quoted in Darley, G., *op. cit.*, p. 181.

57 Quoted in Darley, G., *op. cit.*, p. 116.

58 This was the first Royal Commission to include women
(Beatrice Webb and Helen Bosanquet were also members)
although Gladstone had wanted Octavia on the Royal
Commission on the Housing on the Working Classes in
1884. Unfortunately the Home Secretary of the time had
objected to the absolute impropriety of female
commissioners.

59 Darley, G., *op. cit.*, p. 287.

60 Quoted in Moberly Bell, E., *op. cit.*, pp. 242-43.

61 Brion, M., *Women in the Housing Service*, Routledge: London,
1995, p. 53.

62 This attitude towards women in housing management is
illustrated by the treatment of Kathleen Strange, a member
of SWHEM, who was appointed housing manager in
Tunbridge Wells soon after the Second World War, when the
housing problem was particularly acute. After nine years
Miss Strange was told by the chairman of the housing
committee that she had been so successful she had made
the job big enough for a man, and the committee had
decided to offer her the position of his deputy. Shortly after
this Miss Strange resigned and entered the prison service.

63 Brion, M., *op. cit.*, p. 118.

64 *Ibid.*, p. 211.

65 Peter Clayton, Secretary of the Octavia Hill Society, illustrates this practical approach which characterised the members of SWHEM with a story about a visit to the newly-acquired birthplace of Octavia Hill in Wisbech by Janet Shearman, manager of the Church Commissioners' Octavia Hill Estates. Peter Clayton showed her around the birthplace, which had been acquired in order to turn it into a Museum, and ended his tour by taking Miss Shearman outside and asking her what she thought of it all. 'You need to get those gutters looked at', was her initial response.

66 Daunton, M.J., *op. cit.*, p. 62.

67 According to the Charities Aid Foundation, the 500 top fundraising charities in the UK derive 35 per cent of their income from the state, including national and local government and European funding. [See *Dimensions of the Voluntary Sector: Key Facts, Figures, Analysis and Trends*, West Malling, Kent: CAF, 1997, p. 164.] A recent and comprehensive statistical analysis of the voluntary sector has found that it receives between 35 per cent and 39 per cent of its income from government, depending on how the sector is defined. [Kendall, J., Knapp, M., *The Voluntary Sector in the United Kingdom*, Manchester: Manchester University Press, 1996, p. 111.]

68 *Dimensions of the Voluntary Sector, op. cit.*, p. 55. The extent to which government support of the 'voluntary' sector rises or falls is largely a factor of this single grant. It reached a peak of £2.86 billion in 1992-3, then fell to £2.51 billion in 1993-4. As a result there has been a fall of 10.7 per cent in the level of government support to the sector between 1993-4 and 1994-5, even though grants in most other areas have been increasing.

69 *What Is The Housing Corporation?*, London: The Housing Corporation, undated, p. 7.

70 *Ibid.*, p. 3.

71 'By 1974 the Housing Corporation was approving over 16,000 houses a year through housing associations, over 10,000 of which were new houses for fair rent. Some 5,500 were under the co-ownership scheme.' *Ibid.*

72 This often included an element of public loan finance to make up the difference between the grant and the full capital costs.

73 *Ibid.*, p. 5.

74 'Cracks appear in the Foundations', *Investors' Chronicle*, March 1994.

75 This arrangement is not entirely new. Under the terms of the 1936 Housing Act housing societies were able to borrow money at 2.5 per cent from the Public Works Loan Board, going through their local authority. The local authority would, in turn, require that a certain proportion of the societies' houses would be 'earmarked for tenants nominated by it'. According to Lord Beveridge: 'Mainly for this reason housing societies sometimes prefer to borrow otherwise than through the local authority, using as their main sources either building societies or one or more of the collecting societies'. [Beveridge, *Voluntary Action; A Report on Methods of Social Advance*, London: George Allen and Unwin, 1948, p. 103.]

76 *House Styles: Performance and Pricing in Housing Management*, London: The Audit Commission, December 1996, p. 10.

77 Octavia Hill Housing Trust Financial Statements, 31 March 1997, pp. 8 and 10.

78 Joseph Rowntree Foundation, *Findings: Housing Research 202*, February 1997, summarising *Contemporary Patterns of Residential Mobility in Relation to Social Housing in England*, York: Centre for Housing Policy.

79 Audit Commission, *op. cit.*, p. 11. The reduction of the Housing Association Grant which is payable under the 1988 Housing Act has led to a rise in rents for housing association properties, as the associations now have to repay large-scale loans taken out in the commercial sector [see Sparkes, R., *The Money Game: Money, Charities and the City*, London: Demos, 1995, pp. 14-17]. Rising rents have driven out the better-off tenants, for whom the commercial rented sector becomes more attractive by comparison. Paradoxically, the remaining tenants are most likely to be those who can 'afford' the higher rents because they are claiming Housing Benefit, so a reduction in government expenditure by one

agency is matched by an increase in another, whilst at the same time leading to the creation of welfare ghettos.

In 1996-97 Housing Benefit amounting to £11.1 billion was paid to over four million households in both the housing association and the local authority rented sectors. The Audit Commission estimated that nearly £1 billion of this was lost to fraud. [*Fraud and Lodging: Tackling Fraud and Error in Housing Benefit*, London: the Audit Commission, July 1997.]

80 Moberly Bell, E., *op. cit.*, pp. 282-83.

81 Spicker, P., 'Legacy of Octavia Hill', *Housing*, June 1985, p. 39, quoted in Brion, M., *Women in the Housing Service*, *op. cit.*, p. 16. Chapter Two of Marion Brion's book gives a good account of the changing responses to Octavia's work.

82 Owen, D., *English Philanthropy 1660-1960*, Cambridge: Mass: Harvard University Press, 1965, pp. 386-87.

83 Himmelfarb, G., 'The Age of Philanthropy', *The Wilson Quarterly*, Spring 1997, p. 55.

84 Murray, C. *et al.*, *Charles Murray and the Underclass: The Developing Debate*, London: IEA Health and Welfare Unit, 1996.

85 Field, F., *et al.*, *Stakeholder Welfare*, London: IEA Health and Welfare Unit, 1996.

86 Even Octavia, who was by nature a modest person, was not proof against the pride which consumes all authors when *The Homes of the London Poor* was published to great acclaim. 'My book has been so well reviewed,' she wrote to her friend Sydney Cockerell, 'fourteen reviews in all, and all favourable! I don't now believe it is selling though, it is so dear!' According to Edmund Maurice, Octavia's brother-in-law, the American edition of the book appeared first, followed by the English one in the same year and a German translation two years later [Darley, p. 153]. However she was disappointed by the reception of *Our Common Land* two years later.

87 The first biography (1913) of Octavia was written by her brother in law, Edmund Maurice, son of F.D. Maurice, and consisted of little more than extracts from her letters strung together by a skeletal text. Her niece Elinor Southwood Ouvry published a selection of the letters in 1933 with a Preface by Neville Chamberlain. A collection entitled *The*

Befriending Leader: Social Assistance Without Dependency,
edited by James L. Payne, was published by Lytton Publishing Company, Sandpoint, Idaho, in 1997.